walk

Our Journey Toward Christlikeness

With Study Guide

WALK: Our Journey Toward Christlikeness

Published in 2012
by
College Press Publishing Co.
Printed and bound in the USA

The following is an online discount code that can be used at Harvest Bookstore online in order to download the videos. Please visit www.eastviewchurch.net/walk-videos and add the videos to your shopping cart. Then check out and use the discount code: *walk2012* which will allow you to download the videos for free.

Visit: http://www.eastviewchurch.net/walk-videos
Discount code: walk2012

Thank you to all of the gracious "behind the scenes" support we have received in producing this material. The editing prowess of Susie Baker, Rachael Melvin, and Julie Probst saved me (us) from many distracting grammatical blunders. The artwork of Karen Norris and Scott Sarver continues to amaze me as well. Your creativity and imagery captures the essence of the message with stunning clarity. Content feedback from Jason Sniff and Charlie Welke has been a blessing also. Your encouragement and wisdom have been helpful in developing this resource. Special thanks to the writing team of Mike Baker, Tyler Hari, J.K. Jones, Jason Smith, and Mark Warren. In a busy season of ministry, you found the time to write inspiring devotionals that will equip and encourage thousands of readers! J.K., this project is a reflection of your influence on all of us as we grow in our understanding of spiritual formation. Thank you for coaching me through the framing, phrasing, and oversight of this resource. I trust that you see your fingerprints all over this! Finally, thank you to Mike Baker for the vision to entrust this project to your staff and for your unwavering support and energy for teaching God's Word. We are blessed to be led by a visionary man who is zealous to "walk as Jesus walked."

In Christ,
Jim Probst

Table of Contents

Monday: God the Holy Spirit Takes the Initiative
Tuesday: The Holy Spirit Searches
Wednesday: The Holy Spirit Testifies
Thursday: The Holy Spirit Helps
Friday: The Holy Spirit Intercedes
Saturday: The Holy Spirit Fills

Monday: Through Various Means
Tuesday: Pain
Wednesday: Relationships
Thursday: Service
Friday: Nature
Saturday: Scripture

Monday: In Cooperation with Our Response
Tuesday: Bible Intake / Meditation
Wednesday: Repentance / Confession
Thursday: Witness / Work
Friday: Solitude / Silence
Saturday: Stewardship / Simplicity

Foreword

Jesus' entire recruitment speech for discipleship can be summed up in two words: "follow me." That's it. No "how to" instructions, no list of rules, and no stringent membership qualifications. He was simply interested in anyone who would be willing to do one thing - follow. In first century Galilee the way to learn was for the student (a disciple) to walk with the teacher (a rabbi) who had called him to follow. As the greatest teacher of all time, Jesus naturally called students to walk with Him. His invitation has not changed in twenty centuries.

The study we are beginning together is called "Walk" because we want to be a "fearless church of Christ-followers" and that means walking with Jesus in this spiritual journey called life. The journey can be long, the road is sometimes unpredictable, and there are no short cuts. Yet, if we want to grow in our faith, we are going to have to walk with Jesus, to follow Him over the long haul, and learn from His example.

For the next six weeks we are going to walk with the Jesus of the Bible to learn how He wants us to grow as we follow Him. We will use the following phrase to guide our study: *God the Holy Spirit takes the initiative, through various means, in cooperation with our response, changes us to look like Jesus, in order to serve others, to the glory of God.*

One more important note before we jump in. We walk together. Jesus encouraged disciples to be on journey with Him in company with each other. Our walk is very personal but we should never think of walking alone. We find strength and companionship for the journey in each other and Jesus uses others in the journey to encourage our growth.

I'm blessed to be one of those fellow travelers on this journey. First and foremost I am a follower committed to walking with Jesus all of my life. Second, I am committed to walking by your side as we follow together. It is my prayer that as we spend these few weeks together we will grow together in becoming everything that He has made us to be. Are you ready? Let's go for a walk.

Mike Baker

Sr. Pastor, Eastview Christian Church, Normal, IL

INTRODUCTION

Last fall I joined a crowd of zealous supporters at a local high school football game. I was there primarily to cheer on two different players from opposing teams, hoping not to expose my indifference to the rest of the roster. My son was playing against one of his closest friends in a heated cross-town rivalry. As I scanned the sidelines to find the two boys, I heard something that grabbed my attention. One of our friends noted that she recognized my son's buddy by the way he walked ... not by his number. Our little section of the crowd all understood what she was saying. There was something about his gait that was familiar to us, perhaps even more distinguishing than his frame, the color of his jersey, or the position he played. This is certainly true of many people that we know. A person doesn't need to be physically challenged, injured, or particularly unique in stature to be recognized by their walk. Think about your best friend. My guess is that you could recognize the subtle nuances of his/her walk. You could likely pick them out in a crowded shopping mall just by the way they put one foot in front of the other in their own unique way.

I had noticed something similar on Halloween a few years ago. Even a convincing Spiderman costume that covers a six year old boy from head to toe does not disguise his identity from those who know him well. There's something about the posture, pace, and pattern of his little steps that give away his true identity. I suppose the "masks" that we wear are not much more concealing than the one "Spidy" the neighbor boy wore. From time to time we put on a confident or cheerful face while we limp through the day, hoping nobody will notice. But our walk is more visible and revealing than we realize.

As we cheered on the boys at that football game, I couldn't help but draw the spiritual comparison. There is something about the way we "walk" that is incredibly important. In fact, people might recognize our walk more than our talk, our religious affiliations, and our intentions. As I left the football game that night, I found myself contemplating my own walk. Do people recognize me by more than just my words and intentions? Does my stride declare my dedication and devotion to my Father?

Metaphors are powerful and effective tools for communication. Countless metaphors throughout the Scriptures help us to better understand who we are as Christ followers. "Walk" is a vivid word picture that is masterfully expressed in the book of Ephesians. The word "*peripateō*" is used seven times in this book (97 times throughout the New Testament). It is translated as "live" in the NIV while the KJV, NKJV, NASB, and ESV translators chose the word "walk" to best convey the meaning. The word means to make one's way or to progress; to make due use of opportunities. Notice the following passages in Ephesians where the author compels us to take notice of our "walk."

- "And you were dead in the trespasses and sins in which you once **walked**, following the course of this world." (Eph. 2:1-2a ESV, emphasis mine)

- "For we are his workmanship, created in Christ Jesus for good works, which God prepared beforehand, that we should *walk* in them." (Eph. 2:10 ESV, emphasis mine)

- "I therefore, a prisoner of the Lord, urge you to *walk* in a manner worthy of the calling to which you have been called." (Eph. 4:1 ESV, emphasis mine)

- "Now this I say and testify in the Lord, that you must no longer *walk* as the Gentiles do, in the futility of their minds." (Eph. 4:17 ESV, emphasis mine)

- "And *walk* in love, as Christ loved us and gave himself up for us, a fragrant offering and sacrifice to God." (Eph. 5:2 ESV, emphasis mine)

- "for at one time you were darkness, but now you are light in the Lord. *Walk* as children of light." (Eph. 5:8 ESV, emphasis mine)

- "Look carefully then how you *walk*, not as unwise but as wise." (Eph. 5:15 ESV, emphasis mine)

In this book we will attempt to address the enormous topic of spiritual formation with a simple metaphor and a working definition.

Our hope is that the imagery of "walk" will help us to convey what each of us experiences on this journey of faith. While we aim to advance or clarify our understanding of our spiritual journey, we recognize that this book is a very small tributary in a swelling ocean of resources that help us to grow in our faith. Truthfully, this book only begins the conversation of spiritual formation.

There are many helpful definitions of spiritual formation. The following collection of descriptions and definitions provide an overview of concepts that will help us in our understanding as we narrow the focus to our own definition as it unfolds in the coming chapters. In short, our spiritual formation influences our walk and our walk reveals our spiritual formation. With this in mind, take a moment to familiarize yourself with these insights from some brilliant authors.

- "Spiritual formation is the progressive patterning of a person's inner and outer life according to the image of Christ through intentional means of spiritual growth." (Mel Lawrenz, *The Dynamics of Spiritual Formation,* p. 15)

- "Spiritual formation is a process of being conformed to the image of Christ for the sake of others." (M. Robert Mulholland Jr., *Invitation to a Journey,* p. 12)

- "Spiritual formation in the Christian tradition, then, is a lifelong process through which our new humanity, hidden with Jesus Christ in God, becomes ever more visible and effective through the leading of the Holy Spirit. Spiritual formation at its best has been understood to be at once fully divine and fully human –

that is, initiated by God and manifest in both vital communities of faith and in the lives of individual disciples." (Various Contributors, *The Spiritual Formation Bible,* p. XI)

- "Training in the Spiritual Disciplines is the God-ordained means for forming and transforming the human personality so that in the emergency we can be 'response-able' – able to respond appropriately." (Richard J. Foster, *Life With God,* p. 18)

- "Spiritual formation is the careful attentiveness to the work of God, our master sculptor, as we submit to the gradual chipping away of all that is not of God ..." (Henri Nouwen, *Spiritual Direction,* p. 17)

- "Christian spiritual formation ... is the redemptive process of forming the inner human world so that it takes on the character of the inner being of Christ himself." (Dallas Willard, *The Great Omission,* p. 53)

To this point we've only looked at one side of spiritual formation, assuming that there is an inevitable progression toward Christ over time. There is, however, another side to this story. The painful reality is that formation is not always a positive development toward Christ-likeness. There are practices and situations that can be a hindrance to our "walk." We cannot assume that inactivity or inattention will result in a life transformed into the image of Christ. Sometimes the influences and circumstances of a sin-stained world influence our "walk," leaving us with a spiritual limp or atrophy.

Years ago I was the subject of a hilarious misunderstanding as a new member of a mega church staff. Within the first few months of joining the staff I had the disappointment of injuring my left knee while rescuing three children and a spotted owl from a burning building. Alright, that isn't exactly how it happened, but it sounds far better than the truth! I actually ruptured my left ACL (knee) playing co-ed volleyball in our church league. This was the third time I'd torn my ACL in the past five years.

A couple of weeks after surgery my leg was still quite sore and my range of motion was limited. With the help of a compression bandage and some ibuprofen, I thought I was managing to conceal my woes as I worked through my regular Sunday routine. I later found that a staff member's wife saw things differently. Weaving bits of the story through outbursts of laughter, my co-worker mentioned a brief conversation he had with his wife on Sunday afternoon. "What's up with Jim?" she asked. "What's the deal with that 'cool guy' strut? I didn't expect that from him…" Imagine her surprise when she learned that I was recovering from surgery rather than discovering my new swagger. The misunderstanding was good for a laugh, but the spiritual truth behind this illustration is no laughing matter.

It's not likely that volleyball will become your spiritual downfall. But we do travel through an onslaught of challenges that have the potential to hinder our walk with Christ. Financial stressors, work demands, family life, and a persistent "counter-Christ culture" can cause us to limp, stumble, and fall in our journey. I believe M. Robert Mulholland, Jr. said it best,

> "Spiritual formation is not an option. Spiritual formation is not a discipline just for 'dedicated disciples.' It is not a pursuit only for the pious ... *Spiritual formation is the primal reality of human existence.* Every event of life is an experience of spiritual formation. Every action taken, every response made, every dynamic of relationship, every thought held, every emotion allowed: These are minuscule arenas where, bit by bit, infinitesimal piece by infinitesimal piece, we are shaped into some kind of being. We are being shaped either toward the wholeness of the image of Christ or toward a horribly destructive caricature of that image ... The question is not *whether* to undertake spiritual formation. The question is *what kind* of spiritual formation are we already engaging in? Are we being increasingly conformed to the brokenness and disintegration of the world, or are we being increasingly conformed to the wholeness and integration of the image of Christ?" (*Shaped by the Word*, p. 25-26)

Why all this fuss about spiritual formation? The truth is – we are being formed whether we like it or not. We are being formed "toward the wholeness of the image of Christ" or "toward a horribly destructive caricature of that image." With this in mind, we need to be aware of the Holy Spirit's initiative in our lives and available to partner with Him in growing us to be more Christ-like. To expand on this awareness and availability a bit more, let's look at our working definition of spiritual formation that will serve as an outline for the rest of this book. The architect of this definition is Dr. J.K. Jones, Jr. who serves as Pastor of Spiritual Formation at Eastview Christian Church. His extensive experience and enthusiasm for spiritual formation has become contagious throughout the staff and congregation. Through his influence, we believe that spiritual formation is best addressed in the following way:

Spiritual Formation:

- God the Holy Spirit takes the initiative ...
- through various means ...
- in cooperation with our response ...
- changes us to look like Jesus ...
- in order to serve others ...
- to the glory of God.

In the coming pages, you will see that these six elements of spiritual formation will serve as chapter divisions for this book. While each element will be addressed individually, we recognize that these elements do not stand independently. Rather than a checklist of activities, these elements work in concert with one another as we walk with Him.

As we journey together through this book, I encourage you to commit to the following practices:

- Attend church services weekly (connecting and contributing in community).

- Read this book daily (as a way to establish or continue daily personal devotions).

- Join / attend a small group (completing the corresponding study in the back of this book).

Before we get started I'd like to make one more observation. Henri Nouwen once noted,

> "Ministry is not meant to be done alone but in community. Ministry is not something we have and offer to another in need, but something offered and received in mutual vulnerability and benefit. Ministry is a communal and mutual experience. We don't minister *to*; we minister *with* and *among* others." (*Spiritual Direction*, p. 132)

I couldn't agree more!

This book is a practical application of this very priority of community. Rather than the sole effort of one author, this book is the continuation of a collaborative effort with the pastoral leadership team at Eastview Christian Church. Each chapter of this book will have daily devotions written by Jim Probst (Pastor of Small Groups), J.K. Jones (Pastor of Spiritual Formation), Mike Baker (Senior Pastor), Tyler Hari (Pastor of Outreach), Jason Smith (Pastor of Children's Ministries), and Mark Warren (Executive Pastor). The partnership with these men is absolutely priceless to me. My prayer is that you find this collaborative effort to be richly rewarding for you and your small group as you *walk* together.

WEEK ONE

GOD THE HOLY SPIRIT TAKES THE INITIATIVE

MONDAY

"We love because he first loved us." -1 John 4:19

We number speeches in our house. Number 26 is "I love you ... now leave." This one came in handy back in my youth ministry days when students would try to "out-linger" one another. An hour after the event was over there would still be a dozen teenagers trying to outlast one another - as if there was some sort of victory in being the last to leave the building. Truth be told, #26 was the first speech to receive a number. It gave the impression that there was more to discover along the way and paved the way for some interesting spontaneous "speeches." Speech #13 was taken from an old sitcom. It randomly declares, "Not all Barry Manilow albums sound alike, you're just not listening hard enough!" Other speeches have worked their way into our day-to-day conversations with my kids. Number 3 is frequently cited at the dinner table. It simply says, "Talk to one another as if you actually love one another." Number 2 is "stop mumbling." I'm sure it has nothing to do with my lousy hearing. One of the more common speeches is #9 which comes in handy when any of the kids appears shocked when their newly discovered joke or trick is already known by their dad. This speech, like many of the others, has a bit of hyperbole and a bit of truth – "I'm over 40 years old, I've already been there and done that."

Of course, our Eternal Father can declare most definitively that He's "been there and done that." I love A.W. Tozer's statement in *God's Pursuit of Man* where he notes:

"For all things God is the great Antecedent." (p. 2)

There is no way to discover a place that God has not eternally been (see Psalm 139). Before we know God, we are intimately known by God. And, our very relationship *with* Him was initiated *by* Him in love.

1 John 4:19 succinctly captures the heartbeat of the Gospel story, "We love because he first loved us." From Genesis to Revelation, we see a love story unfolding between God the Father and His children. Our right and loving response to God and others is a reflex of His initiating love for us. Søren Kierkegaard, in his work entitled *Praying to Will One Thing* prays:

"Father in Heaven! You have loved us first, help us never to forget that You are love so that this sure conviction might triumph in our hearts over the seduction of the world, over the inquietude of the soul, over the anxiety for the future, over the fright of the past, over the distress of the moment. But grant also that this conviction might discipline our soul so that our heart might remain faithful and sincere in the love which we bear to all those whom You have commanded us to love as we love ourselves.

You have loved us first, O God, alas! We speak of it in terms of history as if You have only loved us first but a single time, rather than that without ceasing You have loved us first many times and every day and our whole life through. When we wake up in the morning and turn our soul toward You - You are the first - You have loved us first; if I rise at dawn and at the same second turn my soul toward You in prayer, You are there ahead of me, You have loved me first. When I withdraw from the distractions of the day and turn my soul toward You, You are the first and thus forever. And yet we always speak ungratefully as if You have loved us first only once." (Richard Foster, *Devotional Classics*, p. 351)

What a remarkable prayer and perspective. When we think of the initiative of God in our lives, we cannot wander far from His loving disposition that compels His action and calls for our response. Richard Foster clearly expresses this point as he notes:

"From start to finish, God is always the initiator of relationship with us: creating relationship, pursuing relationship, repairing relationship, empowering relationship, consummating relationship. We have freedom to respond as we choose, but first and foremost it is always *God* who acts." (Richard Foster, *Life With God*, p. 23)

Notice the verbs harnessed by Foster to capture the essence of God's initiative (creating, pursuing, repairing, empowering, and consummating). Similarly, the authors of the New Testament employed a variety of words to describe the Holy Spirit's work in the life of the Christ follower. A careful examination of these words might help us to grow in our awareness of His activity in our lives and help us to partner with Him as we make ourselves more readily available. We will discuss our "availabilities" later in the book, but for now let's take a look at the ten primary terms that express the work of the Holy Spirit as He partners with us in our spiritual formation.

The Holy Spirit works within us, through us, and among us in many ways. These ten verbs will be the subject of the video teaching and the remainder of the daily devotionals this week.

NIV	Greek	Teaching
TEACHES	Didasko	Video teaching
REMINDS	Hupomimnesko	Video teaching
GUIDES	Hodegeo	Video teaching
ILLUMINATES	Photizo	Video teaching
CONVICTS	Elencho	Video teaching
TESTIFIES	Martureo	Tuesday devotional
SEARCHES	Eraunao	Wednesday devotional
HELPS	Sunantilambano	Thursday devotional
INTERCEDES	Entunchano	Friday devotional
FILLS	Pletho	Saturday devotional

God the Holy Spirit takes the initiative in our spiritual formation. Our walk is in concert with His *action*. He *acts* as He teaches, reminds, guides, illuminates, convicts, searches, testifies, helps, intercedes, and fills us. We *react*. What is your *reaction* to His loving pursuit of you?

TUESDAY, WEEK ONE

THE HOLY SPIRIT TESTIFIES

*"The Spirit Himself testifies with our spirit that
we are God's children."* -Romans 8:16

Romans 8:16 is a verse so beautiful, so stunningly simple, so full of implications, that I don't quite know where to begin this devotional reflection. This singular verse, comprised of twelve English words, is a mighty river of love - talk spilling over its banks. It is language filled to overflowing with intimacy and affection. Nineteen times in Romans 8, the Apostle Paul intentionally speaks of the ways in which the Holy Spirit is lovingly and faithfully at work in the life of the Jesus-follower. The immediate context of Romans 8, i.e. what comes in front of it (Romans 7) and what comes after it (Romans 9), places *our complete failure* – Paul's, Israel's, all Christians, in the political center of the Roman Empire, other first century believers that would read this letter, mine, and yours – alongside *God's absolute faithfulness*. He, alone, stands as the One and Only Promise Keeper who can always be trusted. Our terrible inadequacy is set alongside His total sufficiency. God has kept His word in providing us an avenue through which we are not rejected, abandoned, and orphaned (Romans 8:1). The Holy Spirit speaks to us of a very special relationship. Notice the verse just in front of 8:16. Paul writes:

"You did not receive a spirit that makes you a slave again to fear, but you received the Spirit of *sonship*. And by Him we cry, '*Abba*, Father.'"

What does that mean? To what specifically is the Holy Spirit testifying?

The Spirit is testifying to us that we have an extraordinarily unique relationship with God. We did not manufacture this idea. It was all His. The Spirit confirms this. He speaks directly, softly, and tenderly of a one-of-a-kind-relationship that has come about through Jesus' death, burial, and resurrection. This is family talk, sweet speech, and passionate adoption language. The word *"testifies"* is something we talk a great deal about at ECC. Our lead pastor, Mike Baker, loves this word. Here's ECC's vision statement: "A fearless church of Christ followers whose ridiculous love and *dangerous witness* are irresistible". *"Testifies"* comes from the Greek word *"martureo."* In the first century a martyr was someone who spoke up, who *gave witness* to something. It's a word that finds its way into the Roman legal system. Originally a martyr was not someone who died for their faith, but someone who told the truth in a court of law. The Spirit *"witnesses"* in God's court that we are uniquely now a part of His family. The fancy word *"sonship,"* back in Romans 8:15 is the starting place. I wish the translators had used the word "adopted" or "adoption" here because that's what Paul is describing – a legal adoption process in God's court. On three other occasions the Scriptures remind us of this colossal truth. Listen:

> "…We wait eagerly for our *adoption* as sons (daughters), the redemption of our bodies." (Here the word is used to describe something we are anticipating at Jesus' Second and Final Return. I know it can seem strange to our ears that adoption is fully engaged now and yet there is even more to come when the new heaven and earth is established and we receive our new bodies. Hallelujah! See Romans 8:23.)

> "Theirs is the *adoption* as sons…" (and daughters – Paul is speaking of his own anticipation of what God will do with the Nation of Israel. See Romans 9:4.)

> "…To redeem those under law, that we might receive *the full rights of sons* (and daughters). Because you are sons, God sent the Spirit of His Son into our hearts, the Spirit who calls out, '*Abba*, Father.' So you are no longer a slave, but a son; and since you are a son, God has made you also an heir." (See Galatians 4:5-7)

Now and then, over the course of a long ministry, I have been asked to speak on behalf of parents wanting to adopt. I can recall the anticipation, the long days growing into weeks, months, and sometimes even years before the adoption process is finally concluded. More than anything, I recall the wide smiles, the holy laughter, the tears of celebration when that child was fully adopted and a part of a brand new family. This is the exact picture Paul uses to describe what the Holy Spirit is speaking into our hearts and minds today. We have been brought into God's family. He longed for us, planned for us, and waited for us. If this doesn't stir our hearts then we have never comprehended the love of God. The Holy Spirit, the grand encourager, is speaking to us this very moment and whispering, "You are my child. I chose you before the foundation of the world." He thought of us before we thought of Him. We **walk** with a loving Father and we **grow** in a loving family. Oh, praise His Name, Father, Son, and Holy Spirit.

Wednesday, Week One

The Holy Spirit Searches

"... but God has revealed it to us by his Spirit. The Spirit searches all things, even the deep things of God." -I Corinthians 2:10

Life is about acquiring knowledge through searching. From an early age we begin asking questions about everything we see. This is why toddlers repeatedly begin their sentences with "why?" We also spend time personally exploring and examining the world around us to figure out how things work. Sometimes we learn the hard way (bees not really liking it when you mess with their nest) and at other times we learn with pleasure (roses smell good and cardinals are pretty). Then we go to school and we begin gathering facts to be stored up in our brains. From addition in math class to sentence structure in English class, we compile an amazing amount of knowledge. The goal of all this learning is to understand. Intelligence is often something we can attain through education and the natural maturing process.

The Christian people of Corinth who first read the above Scripture lived in a culture fully immersed in the world of knowledge, learning, and philosophy. The city was fully Greek and being less than fifty miles from Athens, was strongly influenced by the philosophy and universities of the undisputed center of first century knowledge. The city of Corinth took pride not only in its great wealth and commerce, but also had an air of superiority in understanding and all things intellectual. This may be why they considered "...Christ crucified...foolishness..." (I Corinthians 1:23).

Paul's response was that the knowledge he was talking about was knowledge that only the Spirit of God could search and understand. In essence he was saying: "All your worldly learning and philosophical understandings won't help you in understanding God." He could easily have quoted one of their hero philosophers, Socrates who said, "The only true wisdom is in knowing that you know nothing." Instead he appeals to an understanding of God and things eternal through the "searching" that only the Holy Spirit can do. The Spirit searches all the stuff of God and so (according to Paul) the only hope of truly knowing God is through His Spirit. Forget the wise man. Who needs a smart guy? Why listen to philosophy? All world knowledge not yielded to God is foolishness to His Spirit. (I Corinthians 1:20)

As we follow Christ, the Holy Spirit takes the initiative to grow us by searching the deepest knowledge of God. It's not something we can see or hear or even conceive (I Corinthians 1:9) but God's Spirit gives us all the knowledge of God we need to grow and actually passes it on for our spiritual growth. The word "searches" in this verse is a continuing action and means "to examine through questioning." The Holy Spirit is continuously in touch with God (since He is God) and with us (since He lives in us). This means that we are not left in the dark about God. How does this play out in our everyday life?

God the Spirit continually searches God's deep love through God's Living Word Jesus. There is simply no substitute for faith and devoted following of Jesus as Lord and Savior. The work of the Spirit happens in the lives of followers. This is why people who don't have trust in Jesus often find the things of God hard to understand. They have not accepted God's Word in the flesh and therefore are not led by His Spirit. You must first receive God's Eternal Word before you can move into the deeper stuff of faith. Faith in Christ is the first way the Spirit moves us toward understanding God.

God the Spirit continually searches the direction that God is moving us in our lives, family, and church through prayer. When we pray and ask for God's direction, the Holy Spirit has complete understanding of God's will and passes it on to us. We ask if we should move. We ask who God wants to take a position. We seek direction for our next ministry move. We look for how to spend our resources. We wonder about how to lead our children. We search for our place in the church. We want answers for why things aren't going our way. The

Spirit who lives in us is a cosmic search engine right to the heart of God and gives us answers. How do I know He is giving me direction? Keep praying and His research will be burned on your heart with a peace that is unmistakable.

God the Spirit searches the deep meaning of God through the Bible, God's written Word. Every time a Christ-follower reads the Bible, the Spirit is at work helping us search for God and His wisdom for our lives. I always offer a few simple reminders when reading God's Word that will help us tune into the Spirit's searching. First, start with the straightforward truth of the gospels and the book of Acts. Second, read the Psalms for an understanding of God's heart and how we can pray. Third, no matter what part of the Bible you are reading, look for Jesus in it. Fourth, if you don't understand it, move on and go to something you do understand. Finally, never read the Bible without asking the Spirit to help you understand what you read.

The Spirit helps us examine the deep things of God in many other ways, but these three will get us started. Praise God the Spirit for knowing the deep stuff...and for sharing it with us. He helps us attain wisdom that the smartest men and women of all time cannot understand. Way to go genius! The Spirit...not you.

THURSDAY, WEEK ONE

THE HOLY SPIRIT HELPS

"In the same way, the Spirit helps us in our weakness." -Romans
8:26a

As the gun goes up, the crowd goes silent. The runners crouch down in their blocks, sweat slowly rolls off their faces and crashes onto the track below. Everything leading up to this point becomes obsolete. The chaos of race day, the media blitz, and the surrounding noises are gone. The starter raises his gun, squeezes the trigger, and sends the sprinters exploding out of the block, feet churning, arms pumping, and veins popping. The 100-meter race is one of my favorite track and field competitions. These athletes spend years training their minds and bodies for a ten second race. There are no hurdles, no obstacles, no objects to catch or throw, just 100 meters of wide-open space. Fastest man, or woman wins...see you at the finish line. The 100-meter race reminds us of simpler times, when we looked at a buddy and said, "Race you to the end of the block."

Sometimes, we watch races for entertainment, we participate in them for fun, and even our daily lives feel like a race. We have a name for it, the rat race. It should be no surprise to us then that scripture uses race imagery to describe the Jesus following life. In

Hebrews 12:1, we're reminded to "throw off everything that hinders us and run the race with perseverance." The Apostle Paul encourages us in 1 Corinthians 9:24-27 to "run the race in such a way as to receive the crown that lasts forever." In a moment of reflection, he shares with Timothy in 2 Timothy 4:7 that he has "finished his race."

There's no doubt the image of a race can describe our life's pursuit of Jesus, but let me offer one word of caution. If we think this race is just like the one mentioned above, we're setting ourselves up for failure. Athletes that compete at the highest level of track and field do so because of their physical giftedness and training. No matter how many coaches, sponsors, or supporters they have, when the gun goes off, they're running by themselves. In our race, we run with the Holy Spirit. If we're looking for a mental picture of this type of race, think of a three-legged race. We're bound to the Holy Spirit and we move in step with Him as He helps and guides us.

Think about that for a moment, God the Holy Spirit takes the initiative in our lives to help us! The Holy Spirit helps us in our weakness. What an incredible blessing. At His very core, God, through the Holy Spirit, is for us. If there's one thing that gives us peace, it's in knowing that God actively seeks to help us in our time of need.

The Greek word in Romans 8:26 translated helps is "sunantilambano." That's quite a mouthful! It's actually a combination of three

Greek words sun-anti-lambano. The word "sun" implies a partnership. It's something that we do together. The Holy Spirit comes alongside us and works with us. Talk about a beautiful partnership. The Greek word "anti" means to come against something. It's a passionate word that's very strong in nature. It conveys a righteous anger or rage in the face of evil. God is extremely passionate about our relationship with Him. He loves His children and is against anything that separates us from Him! The final Greek word "lambano" means to take away or receive something.

This word, "sunantilambano," translated helps, reminds us that God the Holy Spirit longs for an active partnership in our lives. We see this in Acts where the power of the church is directly related to the proximity of the Holy Spirit. When we partner with the Holy Spirit, He helps us. When He helps us, our lives are filled with power. When our lives are filled with power, we boldly step out in faith and God works in miraculous ways. If everything in our lives can be explained apart from the work and power of the Holy Spirit, we're not living out our full potential in Christ. In essence, we've entered a three-legged race by ourselves, how foolish!

We're also reminded to think and live in terms of "we" instead of "I." The Holy Spirit longs to advance God's kingdom with us, not for us. To do that would rob us of the life giving experience of walking in step with God. Richard Foster, in his work *Life With God* says it this way:

> "God wants an active partner in relationship. The spiritual life is just that - a life. We learn as we go. We learn as we do. As we go and do with God we're changed along the way. We're called into the struggle and joy of transformation." (p. 134)

How true it is that we're changed along the way because God goes with us. He doesn't cheer us on from the sideline but runs the race alongside us and helps us in our weakness. When we feel tired, overwhelmed, afraid, inadequate, and ineffective, or overlooked we remember that God is the one that takes the initiative in our lives and helps us when we can't help ourselves.

Friday, Week One

THE HOLY SPIRIT INTERCEDES

"In the same way, the Spirit helps us in our weakness. We do not know what we ought to pray for, but the Spirit himself intercedes for us with groans that words cannot express. And he who searches our hearts knows the mind of the Spirit, because the Spirit intercedes for the saints in accordance with God's will." -Romans 8:26-27

As Christ followers, we are not immune to the storms of life. Storms that punch us right in the gut and knock the wind out of our existence. Storms of suffering, sickness, depression, persecution, disappointment, spiritual trials, and grief are a part of life's reality. Storms come in all sizes. Storms can overcome us and bring our current trek to a halt. In these storms it is not unusual to find yourself so overwhelmed that your prayers, which so often roll off the tongue as easy as talking about the latest Bears game, are now found stuck in the recesses of your soul. Prayer is that gift from God that we count on to bring peace and consistency, but now… in some of life's darkest moments… prayers feel as if they fail. We're so consumed by the storms that we don't have the capacity to even muster up a coherent thought to pray. We're not sure what to say or how to say it. Our mind becomes a jumbled thicket of thoughts and emotions, none of which lend themselves to a thoughtful conversation with the very One who can calm the storm.

But take heart, these verses show us that these are fertile times for spiritual formation; times when God the Holy Spirit takes the initiative and intercedes with us in our prayers to help us communicate with God when words and thoughts fail. At these moments, the Spirit directs our prayers to be in line with the very will of God.

I challenge you to read these verses again in view of their context... the present sufferings of God's children. Paul is writing to Christians who are a tested and tattered bunch. Hit by storms on all sides: storms of new faith and tattered pasts, inner-life storms, storms of persecution and betrayal, storms of trials and spiritual struggles...storms not unlike the ones we face today. And in these storms we can count on the Counselor Spirit to guide our prayers from deep within... moans that are without words; moans that come from deep within our souls, initiated by the compassionate work of the Comforter Spirit. As we moan, the Spirit directs our prayerful hearts towards those things which we ought to be praying about. J.K. Jones, our Spiritual Formation Pastor and ninja monk says:

> "Think of this in light of the literary context of Romans [7 and 8], the last part is all about Paul's struggle in the Jesus-following life, his frustration with his own inconsistency, and then on the other side in chapter 9 he reveals his heartache for his own people and how he would willingly exchange his eternity in heaven if they would only come to faith in Jesus. How can you pray for those kinds of challenges unless the Spirit is interceding?"

Many times seated with deep emotion, these moments of wordless prayers are nearly impossible to describe, but unmistakable when they happen. At these moments, we surely enter into a most God-honoring conversation, as these moaning prayers are raw, honest, unrehearsed, and unimpressive to the ear. Our deepest needs bubble up to the surface from the depths of our being, as the Spirit both knows our deepest need and what God has to say about that need. In these times of wordless, moaning prayers, we often find ourselves reminded of, even introduced to, promises from the Scriptures brought to mind by the Mind of the Spirit who speaks to us in our silenced prayers. These are promises of peace, endurance, power, and overcoming. Some of the well-known promises follow these verses in the very same chapter:

> "For we know in all things God works for the good of those who love him…" (vs. 28);
>
> "If God is for us, who can be against us?" (vs. 31); "..we are more than conquerors" (vs. 37);
>
> "[nothing] will be able to separate us from the love of God…" (vs. 39).

In the context of these storms of life, you can claim that these times and circumstances will be redeemed and used to mold you more into the likeness of Christ. While, we might never choose hard times and a struggling prayer life, we would surely not trade the formation that comes from those times. Charles Spurgeon said:

"I pray you never think lightly of the supplications (prayers) of your anguish. That which is thrown up from the depth of the soul, when it is stirred with a terrible tempest, is more precious than pearl or coral, for it is the intercession of the Holy Spirit." (http://www.spurgeon.org/sermons/1532.htm)

SATURDAY, WEEK ONE

THE HOLY SPIRIT FILLS

"Be filled with the Spirit." -Ephesians 5:18

The entire verse reads: "Do not get drunk on wine, which leads to debauchery. Instead, be filled with the Spirit." Many people use this verse to highlight the command of not getting drunk. Although that is true, it is not the main point of this verse. Paul is using the idea of drunkenness to illustrate being filled with the Spirit. Since most people can relate to this, it is not a bad teaching illustration!

The idea here of being filled is one of influence. Again we get this idea from using and/or abusing alcohol. A "DUI" stands for "driving under the influence." In the state of Illinois if your blood alcohol content is at .08 then it is determined that your faculties are not where they should be.

> "If your blood-alcohol concentration (BAC) is 0.08% or higher, you are legally drunk and it is illegal for you to drive. However, if you are driving with a BAC between 0.05 and 0.08, you may still be cited for a DUI if your behavior suggests you are impaired. This is at the discretion of the officer citing you. Even with a BAC of just 0.06, you double your chance of being involved in a fatal accident." http://www.dmv.org/il-illinois/automotive-law

When your blood-alcohol level has reached a certain level you are no longer in control. The alcohol has taken control and is influencing your mind and/or body. Likewise when you are drunk or filled with the Holy Spirit then He is in control of your mind and body. This begs the question: How does one "get filled with the Spirit?"

In the passage Ephesians 5:18-21 the verb "be filled" is a present tense imperative. This means that it is a command and that it is ongoing. It could read like this: "you have, of course, been filled with the Spirit; keep on like that." In other words, the Christian life should be an uninterrupted filling.

Jesus' primary teaching on the Holy Spirit appears in John 14:15-19, 25-27 and John 16:5-16. Sandwiched between these two texts is the following teaching from Jesus:

> "Remain in me, and I will remain in you. No branch can bear fruit by itself; it must remain in the vine. Neither can you bear fruit unless you remain in me. I am the vine; you are the branches. If a man remains in me and I in him, he will bear much fruit; apart from me you can do nothing." John 15:4-5

The Father is the Gardener (15:1), Jesus is the vine. We are the branches. It might be helpful to think of the Spirit as the sap that delivers the nutrients to the plant. It flows from the ground and roots through the plant to keep it healthy. The more the nutrients are flowing through the plant the healthier it is and the more likely it is to produce fruit. What does this look like?

Following Paul's instruction to be filled with the Spirit, he describes five outcomes. These expressions of the Holy Spirit are bolded below.

> "**Speak** to one another with psalms, hymns and spiritual songs. **Sing** and **make music in your heart** to the Lord, always **giving thanks** to God the Father for everything, in the name of our Lord Jesus Christ. **Submit** to one another out of reverence for Christ." (Ephesians 5:19-21).

Because we are connected (have a reverence) to Christ an overflow of expression of the Spirit results in speaking to one another with encouragement, praising God through making music in our hearts (inward and outward), having an attitude of thankfulness, and submitting to other's best interests. Which of these five are in need of further yielding to the Holy Spirit?

The following hymn is one of the oldest hymns in any hymnal, written by an author in the tenth century or earlier. It directly addresses the Holy Spirit and asks Him to come and fill us with joy, love, protection from our enemy, and peace in our lives. Make it your prayer today.

> Come, O Creator Spirit blest,
>
> And in our hearts take up thy rest;
>
> Spirit of Grace, with heavenly aid
>
> Come to the souls whom thou has made
>
> Thou art the Comforter, we cry,

Sent to the earth from God Most High,

Fountain of life and fire of love,

And our anointing from above.

Bringing from heaven our seven-fold dower

Sign of our God's right hand of power

O blessed Spirit, promised long,

Thy coming wakes the heart to song.

Make our dull minds with rapture glow,

Let human hearts with love overflow;

And, when our feeble flesh would fail,

May thine immortal strength prevail.

Far from our souls the foe repel,

Grant us in peace henceforth to dwell;

Ill shall not come, nor harm betide,

If only thou wilt be our guide.

Show us the Father, Holy One,

Help us to know thy eternal Son;

Spirit divine, for evermore

Thee will we trust and thee adore.

WEEK TWO
THROUGH VARIOUS MEANS...

MONDAY

"Communication is a two-way street. And while we revel in the reality that we can always get through to heaven, our concern should be whether our Lord can always get through to us."
(Joseph Stowell, *Who Said That?*, p. 116)

In the previous chapter we learned about how God the Holy Spirit takes the initiative in our spiritual formation. Our walk is in concert with His *action*. He *acts* as He teaches, reminds, guides, illuminates, convicts, searches, testifies, helps, intercedes, and fills us. We *react*. Our awareness of His initiative helps us to partner with Him in our formation. While the previous chapter aimed at addressing the *what*, this chapter addresses the *how* of spiritual formation.

In order to better grasp the *various means* by which God takes the initiative in our lives, let's consider a familiar cultural experience with advertising. Whether you are a marketing guru or a casual consumer darting and dodging through the gauntlet of advertisements, you know the aggressive and intentional tactics of getting the word out on the street. Company campaigns and salespeople hurl solicitations, information, and propositions like junior high kids in a snowball fight. The more the merrier ... and occasionally they hit the target! The "rule of seven" suggests that people need to hear the message at least seven times (often in various ways) before there is successful reception of the message. On one end of the spectrum, the message is a relatively inexpensive grass roots effort with local appeal and a variety of voices reciting the same thing. On the other end, a dominant voice compels the would-be customers from a more visible and central stage. In 2012, companies shelled out an average of $3.5 million dollars for a thirty second spot during the Super Bowl ... $116,666 per second to watch a baby trade stocks from his crib. I wonder what it must feel like to spend that much money, knowing that millions of people will never see the ad due to an untimely bathroom break! In any case, various voices and volumes are employed to capture the attention and the patronage of the hyper-stimulated customer.

While communication can be expensive, miscommunication is even more so. In his book *Come Before Winter*, Charles Swindoll lists a variety of actual quotes taken from insurance forms as people tried to summarize their auto accidents. The miscommunication while explaining the accidents is priceless:

- "Coming home, I drove into the wrong house and collided with a tree I don't have."

- "The other car collided with mine without giving warning of its intentions."

- "The guy was all over the road; I had to swerve a number of times before I hit him."

- "The telephone pole was approaching fast. I attempted to swerve out of its path when it struck my front end."

- "I had been driving for forty years when I fell asleep at the wheel and had an accident."

- "I saw the slow-moving, sad-faced old gentleman as he bounced off the hood of my car."

I get a kick out of these often quoted reports. We can usually connect the dots on these bizarre statements and patch together the author's intent. It's good for a few laughs and the meaning somehow gets through. But what if a critical message remained unheard? What if the means of communication were unrecognized or unavailable?

In the summer of 2002 I found myself perilously perched upon the roof of a rented hostel in Lima, Peru. I wasn't hovering over the exposed re-bar and unfinished concrete because I was star-gazing or enjoying the scenery. I was simply looking for the best reception for a critical nightly check-in with my lovely bride. Three months earlier we were putting the final plans together for our first student ministries mission trip to Lima. A couple dozen families had entrusted the care of their teens to their youth pastor (yours truly) as we journeyed to a new culture and invested in a new partnership with people from a different hemisphere. Well- intentioned parents showed great concern and support as we finished raising support and set the final schedule for our excursion. Meanwhile, there was another journey we were less prepared for.

My mother-in-law had announced her rapidly advancing cancer at Easter of that year. After the initial shock and various treatments, we could see that her time on Earth was limited. As I watched my wife lovingly tend to her mother, I began to see the clash of two commitments. The imminent passing of my mother-in-law was on a collision course with the departure date for this international mission trip. To complicate matters more, my wife was eight months pregnant with our third child! I felt the immense burden to uphold the trust parents had placed in me as the trip leader. Of course, I also knew that the commitment to my wife was non-negotiable. Ultimately, my wife's mother would lose her courageous battle with cancer just days before the trip departure to Peru. After seeking wisdom from trusted friends and wise counselors, I decided to go to Peru (a couple of days late). This decision was finalized only after walking my wife through a painful funeral, receiving her assurance that she would be alright, and assuring her that I would be available day or night via cell phone with no concern for international fees. With this backstory in mind, I made my nightly journey to the ramshackle rooftop.

What I'm trying to express is an example of an absolute commitment to clear communication. The cost was not a barrier. The connection was critical. The communication was absolutely essential. Our relationship warranted the acute awareness of needs and availability to meet those needs. Just in case the correlation isn't crystal clear, the desperate need for communication with a husband in a time of need is much like our dependent relationship with our Father in a sin-stained world.

His creativity in communicating is endless. As we page through our spiritual heritage, we see that He has communicated through a burning bush (Exodus 3:1-6), Balaam's donkey (Numbers 22:28-30), and an angel of the Lord (Matthew 1:20-23; Acts 8:26), just to name a few. Additionally, Jesus made numerous "I AM" statements to express His identity to His followers, including, "I am the bread of life ..." (John 6:35), "I am the light of the world ..." (John 8:12), "I am the good shepherd ..." (John 10:11), "I am the resurrection and the life ..." (John 11:25), and "I am the way, and the truth, and the life ..." (John 14:6). He also paused to ask questions of His often befuddled friends. In Matthew 16:13-15 we see that Jesus asked his disciples, "Who do people say the Son of Man is?" Narrowing the scope, He then asked, "Who do you say I am?" Our Rabbi taught creatively, through various means, with various techniques and tools, to capture the attention and affection of His students. He still does!

At the risk of sharing the obvious, God is a world class communicator. The connection is critical. The cost is great. He purchased access and paved the way to our hearts, not perched upon a Peruvian rooftop, but clinging to a rugged cross (Romans 5:6-11). God the Father is using the finished work of Christ and the ongoing work of the Holy Spirit to capture our attention. He uses various means to reach people with the loving message of salvation. He continues to communicate through various means to cultivate lives that radiate the reality of Christ. Just ask the people in your small group about the creative ways in which God has drawn each of them to Himself. While the cross is central to each story, you will likely hear creative combinations of the five means we will discuss in the coming segments of this book (relationships, pain, service, nature, and Scripture). These are languages that God skillfully and lovingly speaks into our lives to address us in our darkest hours, our most defiant times, and when we are longing for His presence. Our *walk* is dependent upon clear communication, and God is speaking. Are we listening? Are we aware of His means of communication with us?

The remainder of this chapter is devoted to the *various means* by which the Author of Life *takes the initiative* in our lives.

- PAIN

- RELATIONSHIPS

- SERVICE

- NATURE

- SCRIPTURE

These are among the most common ways in which God captures our attention. While this is not an exhaustive list, I trust that discussing these five avenues for communication will help us to open our ears and anticipate how God might be communicating with us. After all, when the King of Kings is calling for our attention, we do well to wade through every competing voice to hear Him and to follow His lead.

Admittedly, one of the greatest avenues for communication with God is through the spiritual disciplines. These disciplines are so rich and so significant that we've dedicated the third chapter of this book to discussing twelve of them. We have also pulled together an extensive sampling of the disciplines in the appendix of this book. These disciplines are ways in which we demonstrate our availability to God. For now, we'll continue to emphasize our awareness of His initiative in our lives as we examine His willingness to communicate through pain, relationships, service, nature, and Scripture.

TUESDAY, WEEK TWO

THROUGH THE MEANS OF PAIN

"Consider it pure joy, my brothers, whenever you face trials of various kinds, because you know that the testing of your faith develops perseverance. Perseverance must finish its work so that you may be mature and complete, not lacking anything...Blessed is the man who perseveres under trial, because when he has stood the test, he will receive the crown of life that God has promised to those who love Him. When tempted, no one should say, 'God is tempting me.'" -James 1:2-4 and 12-13

People have been asking for millennia, "Why is there pain in the world?" "Why doesn't God do something?" The Bible does not hesitate to talk about the reality of pain. It is first introduced when Adam and Eve sin in the Garden of Eden. Genesis 3:1 tells us that when the ancient serpent, Satan, challenged the Lordship of God, "Did God really say, 'You must not eat from any tree in the garden?'" a whole universe was shaken. Confidence in God was lost. An intimate walk with Him was forfeited for a bite of fruit. A life of growing daily in love with God was exchanged for a nibble of pleasure ("the fruit of the tree was good for food and pleasing to the eye" – Genesis 3:6). The result was pain. Pain entered the world and everything and everyone was affected. Three demonic lies were believed: the love of God was presented as envy; service to God was presented as slavery; and life with God was presented as losing out on real life. What the enemy tricked Adam and Eve into believing was – God was not good, loving, and trustworthy. Satan portrayed God as a selfish schmuck who was in the business of depriving people of genuine life.

So, why are there oceans of pain in the world? First of all, Genesis 3 answers that question with one word – "sin." God did not create this world of suffering. We did. It is vitally important to take ownership of that truth. But, and this is huge, God is more than able to redeem it. So much of the Scriptures wrestle with the problem of pain. So much of suffering is framed in stories of "bad things happening to good people." Just saying the name "Job" floods the mind with pictures of suffering that cannot be overlooked. Consider the deeply personal and real pain of righteous prophets like Jeremiah and Isaiah. Contemplate Daniel in the lion's den. Meditate on Joseph waiting in an Egyptian prison. Ponder all those who rushed toward Jesus with crippled hands and feet, blinded eyes, and bodies wrecked by the evils of leprosy. The Bible does not hide from pain. God faces the brutality of suffering at the cross. Talk about innocent!

There is a New Testament writer who seems most in touch with the sticky and thorny "why" of pain. His name is James, the half-brother of Jesus, the writer of a small letter toward the end of the Bible, "Old Camel Knees," as he was called, due to hardened calluses that had formed on his knees from long and persistent praying.

That very James, the one quoted at the start of this devotional, offers some insight into why there is pain and what God intends to do about it. This very wise Jesus-follower uses three distinct words to offer a partial answer to "the why" question. James acknowledges that we face *trials.* Trials are a result of living in a sin-fallen-world (1:2&12). He carefully takes us back to Genesis 3. He admits that we encounter *temptations.* Temptations are a result of living in a world ruled by Satan (see 1:13-14). Finally, James uses the word *tests.* Tests are a result of living in a world so loved by God that He longs for us to be shaped into Jesus' likeness (1:3 & 12). James says God uses "trials of many kinds" (1:2). These pain-filled experiences are multi-faceted. They are diverse, intricate, and complex. The enemy longs to use these trials to devour us, while God desires to use those same trials to grow us. No one escapes trials, temptations, and tests. It is alright to scream to God, "Why is this happening to me?" God is not offended by honest talk. What does offend Him is the way we quickly dismiss pain. It is a paradoxical gift no one wants. God's pain at the cross bloomed into our joy.

I know it seems profoundly insensitive to declare that God can take what the enemy intended for harm and now intend it for good. Cancer, AIDS, abuse of all kinds, divorce, ALS, Alzheimer's, assorted other diseases, murder, rape, death, and a billion other evils can and will be redeemed by God. Even as I write that sentence, I weep for those who are in a terrible season of pain. What James is teaching is shocking – God uses pain as a tool to glorify Himself and mature us. Pain and spiritual growth are inseparable. If you don't believe me, take one more look at the cross.

WEDNESDAY, WEEK TWO

THROUGH THE MEANS OF RELATIONSHIPS

"Honor your father and mother, so that you may live long in the land the Lord your God is giving you." -**Exodus 20:12**
"If one falls down, his friend can help him up."
-**Ecclesiastes 4:10**
"The Lord God said, 'It is not good for man to be alone. I will make a helper suitable for him." -**Genesis 2:18**

These verses may seem like an overload for you today, but I wanted to find something from the Word that spoke to the most common relationships in the human experience. Most of us have a mom and dad or a parental figure in our life, so commandment number five is relevant to each one. Most everyone has at least one friend, so the verse from Solomon's reflections on his life seemed to fit our discussion. And, many who desire to do so will get married, meaning the relationship between husband and spouse should be considered. Parents, children, friends, and spouses are the foundational relationships in our lives and the Holy Spirit uses each of them to grow us into Christ-likeness.

In the listing of the Ten Commandments that God gave to Moses on the mountain, the command for relationship with one's parents is sandwiched in between four initial commandments for relating to God and five commandments for getting along with one's fellow man. This is likely an intentional placement since the proper place for learning both worship of God and relationship with others is the home.

I was doubly blessed to grow up in a Christian home. I learned to pray, sing worship songs, read the Bible, and love the church at a very young age (even though I got a spanking almost every week for acting up in church). My mom and dad laid a firm foundation of faith for my life. I also learned at home about getting along with others: how to share, submitting to authority, working together, punishment for wrongdoing, loving intimately, laughing, fellowship, and communication to name a few. The Holy Spirit definitely grew me through the lives of Bob, Susie, Angie, and Steve. The journey we took together growing up just seemed like normal to me, but the Spirit of God arranged the setting and the lessons learned along the way.

Before I go on, I can just imagine some of you making the proverbial finger-in-mouth gagging sign. Truth is, for many people the idea of mom or dad or home is simply not pleasant. Some have had childhoods which are littered with bitter, even abusive and scary memories. In fact, if you consider anyone to have the perfect family (including mine) you are mistaken. Our family experienced arrest, betrayal, poverty, and separation in our most challenging moments. But the Spirit even used those things to form who I am in Christ Jesus. I don't think God wants us to stay in abusive situations and I don't think an adult child has to pretend like everything was fine growing up. I do think that even the worst of situations can be redeemed by the Holy Spirit to make us more like the Christ-followers we want to become.

God, the Spirit also uses friendships to shape, mold, and sharpen us. Like the wisdom writing says above, friends are really great to have in hard times, but they're good for so much more. A friend can encourage you when you lose the little league championship game, understand you when no one else seems to know how you feel, help you when the storms of life blow your chimney off the roof of your house (true story...thanks Al!), laugh at your silly jokes, and shoot straight with you when they think you are wrong. Friends help form us into the people we are.

Growing up my friend Mike helped me find humor in things and my friend Tommy helped me walk with Christ. My friend Cal has helped me make major ministry and leadership decisions and my friend John has helped me become a better man of God. My friends Stephanie and Al allow me to be who I am and the friends I work with on staff at church encourage me and help me grow. Again, if this sounds like a utopic Mr. Rogers gone wild, you're not getting the full picture. I've had some friends who were not good influences or hurtfully turned on me in the end. These were not pleasant experiences, but the point is that somehow, the Holy Spirit is at work in all my friendships, harvesting what He can for His good purposes in my spiritual life.

The most intense friendship relationship there is comes between husband and wife. God did not like that His created man, Adam, was alone and he had the perfect remedy. He created woman and in so doing established the most life-altering union humans can experience together. Spouses are united in every way possible spanning the full scope of human experience. Marriage is physical, mental (some more mental than others), spiritual, and emotional. To be married is to share in the most intimate way and the Spirit is at work in this community where two become one to spiritually form both. Again, I have been blessed with a great wife who has made me a better man by far. Somehow, the Holy Spirit has used her to keep me balanced, in check, accountable, and free to be myself.

I am not unaware of the growing fragmentation of this wonderful relationship in our culture and how easily people opt for divorce. However, in all these years of ministry I have never met a couple who did not at least experience some of their greatest moments and growth in this God-ordained relationship. Many realize later in life that it was the immaturity and selfishness of both parties that led to the divorce in the first place. Even though the Holy Spirit does not like divorce, He even uses that experience to grow each as they place their faith in Christ. There are of course, marriages that continue to limp along in an unhealthy state. The Holy Spirit can often do His best work through Christian counselors and therapists. At any rate, the Spirit's passion for unity directs His power towards restoration and renewal in all marriages.

This is a small sampling of relationships in our lives, but they are the basic ones for us all. Some relationships we choose and others are chosen for us but we can be sure that the Spirit uses them all to help us grow. Since relationships ultimately shape so much of our personalities, our attitudes, and our views on God; the Holy Spirit works through them to accomplish God's will. It may be helpful today to ask what relationships have most formed your life (for good or bad) and how you think the Spirit has helped you mature spiritually through them.

THURSDAY, WEEK TWO

THROUGH THE MEANS OF SERVICE

"Then Samuel said, 'Speak, for your servant is listening.'"
-I Samuel 3:10

Before Samuel was even born, he was consecrated to the Lord and set apart for His service. Samuel would grow up to become an amazing man of God, prophet, and leader for the people of Israel. Samuel grew up ministering before the Lord at the temple alongside Eli the priest. In those days, a word from the Lord was rare. People were hungry to hear from God, maybe you can relate. Yet we see in this incredible story a God who pursues a young boy, not once, not twice, but three times. The third time God speaks and Samuel, prompted by Eli, utters six simple words. "Speak, for your servant is listening."

This prayer reminds us that God's in the business of speaking as we serve. Samuel prayed this while lying in his bed surrounded by the stillness of the night; we can pray it in the chaos of our day. Samuel served God in the temple; we serve in a variety of places and in a variety of ways. God pursued and spoke to a young boy, how much more is He willing to use you and me if we're available and listening. A life of service has a way of opening a previously disconnected line with God. As we serve, we die to ourselves. All those little needs, wants, and supposed rights our flesh cries out for are emptied out and in return, God fills us with Himself. He, by His very nature, permeates all of life including our service. "Where can I go from your Spirit? Where can I flee from your presence?" (Psalm 139:7)

As we serve, He speaks and as He speaks we're strengthened. Our enemy Satan doesn't want us living lives of service that glorify God and usher in His Kingdom. He doesn't want us hearing clearly from our Maker, so He tries to plant subtle lies in our hearts. In our weaker moments, we're tempted to believe them. The first is to assume that a life of service is the culmination of a fully "arrived" spiritual life. We mistakenly assume that serving others can only come from a near perfect spiritual life. We think our own weaknesses disqualify us from serving others, so we opt out of God's call on our lives (Matthew 20:25-28). Nothing could be farther from the truth. God shapes us as we go and speaks to us as we serve.

The second lie that creeps into our hearts is the subtle belief that our feelings should dictate our actions and not vice versa. How often do we miss God's beautiful voice because we don't feel like serving? We allow feelings, or lack thereof, to drive our level of obedience, when in fact, obedience in spite of our feelings is what drives us closer to God and transforms us most into the image of Christ. As children grow, one marker on the road to maturity is demonstrated perseverance to push forward when feelings begin to wane. We're most ready to hear God's voice through our service when we realize we're not disqualified by our weakness and we're not held hostage by the ebb and flow of feelings.

Throughout Scripture, the type of servant God regularly spoke to was the one focused and faithful in the small acts of everyday service. God will not use us, or speak to us through serving if we deem small opportunities to serve as too trivial, unimportant, or unrecognized. Frances de Sales reminds us that large and small acts of service are like sugar and salt. Sugar may have a more exquisite taste, but its use is less frequent. Salt is found everywhere. Our desire to do great things for God may be a great virtue, but those opportunities are far less frequent. The opportunity to serve others in small ways is a daily choice. Jesus candidly reminds us in Matthew 5:13 that "you are the salt of the earth."

It feels counter-intuitive to think God speaks clearly to us while we serve others. When serving others, our focus isn't on ourselves but other people, and we hardly expect to hear from God then. Yet, that's right where God wants us! As we serve others, God speaks to us about previous hurts, future decisions, present anxieties, and areas of growth in our lives. As we serve others, we loosen the grip on our own personal agendas with God and make room for Him... and God speaks.

FRIDAY, WEEK TWO

THROUGH THE MEANS OF NATURE

"Blessed is he whose help is the God of Jacob, whose hope is in the Lord his God, the Maker of heaven and earth, the sea, and everything in them – the Lord, who remains faithful forever." -
Psalm 146:5-6

As I compose this devotional thought, it's springtime here in Central Illinois and a cool breeze blows across my face as I hear nothing but the playful songs of the robins and the mournful coos of the doves. The glow of the morning sun is illuminating a low fog dancing off the water of this secluded pond. A stubborn full moon hangs in the southwest, unwilling to let the night slip away. A deep blue western sky fades easterly to a fresh blue background, as the earliest rays of light kiss the edges of the clouds, frosting them with iridescent shades of purplish-pink. The smell of lilacs fills the air as rabbits get in a quick game of tag before they return to their burrows in the long grass…and I breathe in this sight as though it were the very breath of all life and I thank God for the peace and beauty of this morning. I must thank Him… not just because my heart is brimming with a great awe mixed with joy as a child-like wonder dances in my heart, but because I'm the only one who might see this. It would be a shame if no one thanked God for making this morning! I dare not say too much, for fear of ruining the moment, but the wordless prayers of my heart sing the praises of our Creator.

Why is it that nature has such a connection to our heart? What is it about the beauty of creation that grabs our attention and opens the windows to our soul? As a part of His creation, deep emotions are inexplicably awakened by the grandeur and detail of the universe around us. Beyond the emotional connection, there is great fascination in the intellectual discoveries of the world. Science, as much as art and music, is an expression of worship as we delight in the works of God's hands. How fascinated we are by the study of His work, whether the breathtaking views of the far sides of space through our most powerful telescopes, or the staggering details of the intelligent design of DNA.

Imagine David spending his nights in the fields with his sheep in ancient Palestine. The views he must have seen with no city lights to drown out the beauty, as the expanse from horizon to horizon displayed heavenly scenes of God's splendor. No doubt scenes like these played in his thoughts as he penned words such as those found in Psalm 8:3-4:

> "When I consider your heavens, the work of your fingers, the moon and the stars, which you have set in place, what is man that you are mindful of him, the son of man that you care for him?"

Nature communicates. It speaks to us through avenues not limited by words. It points us to God and reveals His eternal power and divine nature (Romans 1:18). It counsels us to put our trust in God rather than our own means - we don't look half as good as a field of lilies, though they just rely on God for their existence (Matthew 6:25-34). Nature reveals commonsense ways to live life, such as "if you don't work, you don't eat" (Proverbs 6:6-11). Nature reminds us that God is the God of all, and in His great care and incomprehensible grace, shows kindness to this broken creation (Matthew 5:43-48). Nature reminds us of who we are and our place within this planet as caretaker and authority (Genesis 1:28-31). It also reminds us of who we are and are *not*, by the vastness and wisdom of all creation. Job knows this all too well as we read God's challenge to Job in Job 38 and 39. Like Job, have we considered that we were not there when creation began, when the ocean was marked off, or when light came forth from God's lips? Are we aware when a baby doe is born in the middle of a forest, or when and where lightning will strike? Can we fill the night sky with stars or command eagles to soar? In humility, we find that nature reminds us every day that God is on His throne and we are blessed when we have our help and hope in the Maker of heaven and earth (Ps. 146:5). God the Holy Spirit takes the initiative and uses nature in his sanctifying work of conforming us to the Creator's image.

SATURDAY, WEEK TWO

THROUGH THE MEANS OF SCRIPTURE

"The law of the Lord is perfect, reviving the soul. The statutes of the Lord are trustworthy, making wise the simple. The precepts of the Lord are right, giving joy to the heart. The commands of the Lord are radiant, giving light to the eyes." -Psalm 19:7-8

Have you ever received a love letter? Maybe you received one as a junior high student when a person of the opposite sex first revealed they liked you. Or maybe a parent sent you a note when you left home telling how much they loved you; or perhaps your child wrote how much you mean to them. Maybe you received an encouraging note on a birthday card from a friend. What do we do with these? Who reads the note once and throws it away? You keep the note in a safe place and read it over and over and over again. The love letter fills us with feelings of hope, significance, joy, and love.

One of the best ways to describe the Bible is God's love letter. He has written a personal love letter to each of us describing how much He loves us and how He wants a relationship with us. It is filled with stories, questions, prophesies, commands, and poetry. The Bible is meant to be read more like a love letter than a newspaper or period-ical. *"What other book can you read and at the same time talk to the author about it?"* (Gene Appel)

The Psalms are filled with miniature love letters to God and from God. They reveal raw emotions and life changing truths. In particular Psalm 19:7-8 showcases four (shown in italics) amazing truths about God's Word and four life-changing promises when we believe these truths.

"The law of the Lord is perfect, reviving the soul."

The Message translation captures the essence of this verse by saying it this way:

"The revelation of God is whole and pulls our lives together."

God's Word is complete. It is not lacking anything. It gives the entire picture of who He is, who we are, and His plan to save us. It brings revival, renewal, and redemption. It is good and true. Like God, it is perfect. Sin and death are replaced with forgiveness and life. This truth should revive our souls. What part of your soul needs renewal today? Scripture always accomplishes that.

"The statutes of the Lord are trustworthy, making wise the simple."

God is faithful. He does not break His Word. He keeps His promises. His plans and purposes are best. His directions are accurate. Scripture always tells the truth.

"Counsel and sound judgment are mine." (Prov. 8:14)

We are simple like children. We can be foolish and need wisdom.

We need guidance and direction and God's Word always provides.

"Sin will keep you from this book or this book will keep you from sin." *(Dwight L. Moody)*

"In all your ways acknowledge him and he will make your paths straight." (Proverbs. 3:6)

"You guide me with your counsel and afterward you will take me into glory." (Psalm 73:24)

Where do you need wisdom today? Scripture always provides the necessary help.

"The precepts of the Lord are right, giving joy to the heart."

God's Word is not simply true but it is truth itself. The Bible is not simply true in the sense that it conforms to some higher standard of truth, but rather the Bible is the final standard of truth. There is great comfort and security in not only knowing what is true but who is truth ... Jesus! This kind of confidence brings deep and everlasting joy.

"The ordinances of the Lord are sure and altogether righteous. They are more precious than gold . . . and sweeter than honey." (Psalm 19:9-10)

"I delight in your commands because I love them." (Psalm 119:47)

Do you love reading the Bible? Try reading it recreationally . . . like a novel. Scripture is inviting.

"The commands of the Lord are radiant, giving light to the eyes."

Jesus is the light of the world. In Jesus is life and that life is the light of mankind. (John 1:5) He has conquered darkness. We were spiritually blind but now we see. His words provide illumination to the darkness in our souls. He provides clarity and understanding to guide our steps.

> "Your word is a lamp unto my feet and a light for my path." (Psalm 119:105)

Through the Bible we can find our purpose and gain understanding on the direction of our lives. Scripture is God's primary tool in transforming us to look like Jesus.

> "Most people are bothered by those passages in Scripture that they cannot understand. The Scripture which troubles me most is the Scripture that I do understand." (Mark Twain)

Where do you need guidance today?

The following hymn speaks of the promises of God's word. Make this hymn your prayer today.

> Standing on the promises of Christ my King,
>
> Through eternal ages let his praises ring!
>
> Glory in the highest I will shout and sing
>
> Standing on the promises of God!

Chorus:

Standing, standing, standing on the promises of God my Savior;

Standing, standing, I'm standing on the promises of God.

Standing on the promises that cannot fail

When the howling storms of doubt and fear assail;

By the living Word of God I shall prevail

Standing on the promises of God!

Standing on the promises of Christ the Lord,

Bound to him eternally by love's strong cord,

Overcoming daily with the Spirit's sword

Standing on the promises of God!

Standing on the promises I cannot fall,

Listening every moment to the Spirit's call,

Resting in my Savior as my all in all

Standing on the promises of God!

Author: R. Kelso Carter, 1886

WEEK THREE

IN COOPERATION WITH OUR RESPONSE ...

MONDAY

"Do you not know that in a race all the runners run, but only one gets the prize? Run in such a way as to get the prize. Every one who competes in the games goes into strict training. They do it to get a crown that will not last; but we do it to get a crown that will last forever. Therefore I do not run like a man running aimlessly; I do not fight like a man beating the air. No, I beat my body and make it my slave so that after I have preached to others, I myself will not be disqualified for the prize." **-1 Corinthians 9:24-27**

I love the Olympics. There's something inspiring about watching the very best of the best compete on the world's largest stage. The intensity is heightened when you consider the miniscule window of opportunity for these remarkable athletes. Most often there is only a matter of seconds to demonstrate the mastery of their craft. Sickness, injury, nervous jitters, or a momentary lapse of concentration during their moment in the spotlight could jeopardize a literal lifetime of training. While there is an occasional meltdown or malfunction captured on camera, the overwhelming characterization of these Olympians is their radical transformation from ordinary to extraordinary. Their accomplishments appear beyond the realm of human achievement.

Whether we're talking about a pint-sized gymnast, a burly shot put champion, or a sleek marathon runner, there is a common appreciation for the kind of transformation that only takes place by a lifetime of dedicated training. Time alone does not produce this kind of metamorphosis. Training methods, nutrition, coaching, and relentless dedication all translate to measurable change for the athlete who perseveres. I'm inspired by their example, but I cannot truly relate to that kind of training.

At the far end of our basement we have the kind of workout equipment that you'd find lingering at the curb at the end of a garage sale. I occasionally muster the courage to enter into this little room with one of my kids so that we can grunt out a few exercises and discuss lofty fitness goals. There are no Olympic aspirations here, just an opportunity to bond with my kids and to stave off the advancement of my ambitious waistline.

A couple of years ago I scribbled two little phrases on the unfinished wall in this little room. The first is 1 Timothy 4:8 which reads: "For physical training is of some value, but godliness has

value for all things, holding promise for both the present
life and the life to come."

The second is one simple phrase – "athletae dei." This Latin term
means "athlete of God," suggesting that Christianity calls for much
more than being a spectator. The Apostle Paul captured this concept
of spiritual training for the "athletae dei" most vividly in 1 Cor. 9:24-
27 (quoted at the beginning of this chapter). In this passage, Paul
describes the kind of commitment necessary to compete in the
Isthmian games (similar to the Olympic games with which we are
more familiar). This metaphor of training is one of many Paul uses to
compel the church to intentionally train themselves in righteousness.
Our basement graffiti has been a launching pad for discussion and
thought over the past two years. It has helped us to consider the value
and effort placed on physical training in comparison to spiritual training. While we may never grace the stage of Olympic glory, our spiritual journey has begun and we are in training.

As we've read and discussed in the first two chapters, our *walk* is
an elaborate partnership with God for our spiritual formation. We recognize that He takes the initiative, through various means, so that we
might look more like Jesus. But this initiative must be *in cooperation
with our response*. In his book *Life With God*, Richard Foster notes:

"Our inner world (the secret heart) becomes the home of
Jesus, by his initiative and our response. As a result, our

interior world becomes increasingly like the inner self of Jesus, and, therefore, the natural source of the words and deeds that are characteristic of Him. By his enabling presence we come to 'let the same mind be in you that was in Christ Jesus.'" (Phil. 2:5) (p. 10)

While our first two chapters addressed our awareness of God's work, this chapter and the following chapter address the other side of the same coin: our availability in this partnership of our formation.

What we're really talking about is creating space in our lives for God's influence to take root. Generally speaking, these *availabilities* are known as spiritual disciplines. Perhaps the best way to move forward is to look back at some foundational thoughts Christian authors and leaders have expressed regarding the spiritual disciplines:

- "Spiritual Discipline: Any activity that can help me gain power to live life as Jesus taught and modeled it." (John Ortberg, *The Life You've Always Wanted,* p. 47)

- "I will maintain that the only road to Christian maturity and Godliness (a biblical term synonymous with Christlikeness and holiness) passes through the practice of the Spiritual Disciplines." (Donald S. Whitney, *Spiritual Disciplines for the Christian Life,* p. 14)

- "Training in the Spiritual Disciplines is the God-ordained means for forming and transforming the human personality so that in the emergency we can be "response-able" – able to respond appropriately." (Richard Foster, *Life With God,* p. 18)

- "The Disciplines allow us to place ourselves before God so that he can transform us." (Richard Foster, *Celebration of Discipline,* p. 7)

- "Anything and everything we do can be a spiritual discipline if we offer it to God as a means for God to use in our lives if God so chooses. 'Doing' becomes 'being' when we offer our 'doing' to God and keep offering it as a means for God to do whatever God wants to do in and through our lives." (M. Robert Mulholland Jr., *Shaped by the Word,* p. 114)

- "Now, a discipline is an activity in our power, which we pursue in order to become able to do what we cannot do by direct effort." (Dallas Willard, *The Great Omission,* p. 86)

This week you will be introduced to a variety of spiritual disciplines through our video teaching, our daily devotions, and the small group study in the back of this book. Here is a quick snapshot of the daily reading and video teaching addressed this week:

DAILY READING: Personal Spiritual Disciplines

- "in cooperation with our response ..."   Monday

- Repentance / Confession   Tuesday

- Bible Intake / Meditation   Wednesday

- Witness / Work   Thursday

- Silence / Solitude   Friday

- Stewardship / Simplicity   Saturday

VIDEO TEACHING: Corporate Spiritual Disciplines

- Baptism / Communion

- Celebration / Worship

- Fellowship / Confession

There is no exhaustive list of disciplines, but these resources should help to lay the foundation for ongoing availability to God. I encourage you to consider these disciplines as a means of creating space for His work as you cooperate with Him in your spiritual formation. By God's grace, these new holy habits will help you to *walk*, conforming you to the likeness of the Son (Rom. 8:29).

My mind returns to a familiar snapshot from the Olympics where the national anthem is played as an athlete stands at attention to receive his/her reward. It is absurd to think that anyone would regret the training and the discipline behind the scenes of their reward. By faith, I anticipate a far superior ceremony one day. I long for that day when the training and the trials of this life are eclipsed by the splendor of our heavenly reward. On that day we will not regret the training of today. On that day we will see that our holy habits culminate as we enter our new holy habitat called Heaven. As we move into another week of activity, let Mulholland's honest prayer guide your availabilities:

> "God of our creation and re-creation, you who are constantly at work to shape me in the wholeness of Christ, you know the hardness of the structures of my being that resist your shaping touch. You know the deep inner rigidities of my being that reject your changing grace. By your grace soften my hardness and rigidity; help me to become pliable in your hands. Even as I read this, may there be a melting of my innate resistance to your transforming love." (M. Robert Mulholland, Jr., *Invitation to a Journey*, p. 25)

TUESDAY, WEEK THREE

REPENTANCE AND CONFESSION

"On the twenty-fourth day of the same month, the Israelites gathered together, fasting and wearing sackcloth and having dust on their heads. Those of Israelite descent had separated themselves from all foreigners. They stood in their places and confessed their sins and the wickedness of their fathers. They stood where they were and read from the Book of the Law of the LORD their God for a quarter of the day, and spent another quarter in confession and in worshiping the LORD their God." -Nehemiah 9:1-4

I don't know who coined the phrase, "Confession is good for the soul," but I agree. And so does Scripture. God delights in forgiving and restoring. I can't contemplate confession and not have my mind race to repentance. The two go together, inseparable practices. Repentance ushers in confession and confession encourages more repentance. Years ago, in my second year of Bible College, I took a class called "Conditions for Revival." It was a course designed for upperclassmen, but I was eager and didn't want to wait. With the professor's blessing I dug deeply into the reading and writing. I discovered that real revival is marked by a genuine conviction of sin, *an authentic repentance* from sin, *a true confession* of sin, an intentional decision to begin again, an honest trust in God's willingness to forgive, and an active desire to share this Good News with others. Joy is recovered. I know that's a lot to take in, but only repentance and confession matter for this devotional reflection.

The passage quoted above from Nehemiah 9 comes out of the story of Israel's return to the Promised Land, specifically to Jerusalem. The nation had been in exile due to her sins. The city had been destroyed in 586 BC (2 Chronicles 36:181-19). In the Biblical Story it is now 445-444 BC. The broken down walls of Jerusalem have been miraculously rebuilt in fifty-two days (Nehemiah 6:15). Now a different kind of building was required, a rebuilding of the inner life. Repentance and confession were needed. Scholars suggest that anywhere from thirty to fifty thousand have come to Jerusalem in order to celebrate the Feast of Tabernacles. These returning exiles have settled back into the land, an assembly has been called in Jerusalem, Ezra the scribe has been instructed to bring the Law before the assembly, and have it read aloud and interpreted (Nehemiah 8). Don't miss it – Israel asked for the Law to be read aloud, Ezra and other Levites do exactly that while explaining its meaning. And revival broke out. The evidence is in the expression of repentance and confession (Nehemiah 9). They confessed their sins and decided to live in a God-honoring way.

Repentance and confession are mighty spiritual warfare weapons. They destroy the last stronghold of self-justification. Many of us know that our bloodiest and most challenging battles take place at this level. We wage war against the Devil's schemes. He wants us to remain trapped in self-righteous deception or a swamp of self-pity. Repentance is at the very core of what it means to be a Jesus-follower. We acknowledge that our sin cost Jesus His life. He lovingly offered His own body as a perfect sacrifice. Admittedly, confession can also include praise to God as in Hebrews 13:15:

> "Through Jesus, therefore, let us continually offer to God a sacrifice of praise – the fruit of lips that *confess* His name."

Beyond even that, confession can include a faith declaration, like in Romans 10:9:

> "That if you *confess* with your mouth, 'Jesus is Lord,' and believe in your heart that God raised Him from the dead, you will be saved."

Repentance and confession are the prelude to revival and spiritual growth.

Typically we consider these disciplines a private matter between God and ourselves. This is true, but not the whole truth. Repentance and confession are both private and community disciplines. We are fractured and sinful people alone and together (Isaiah 53:6; Romans 3:23, and 1 John 1:8). Sin has the imprisoning capacity to place us in solitary confinement. The truth is that repentance and confession are expressions of God's absolute love for us. He makes a way of escape from the cell block of un-repented and un-confessed sin. These twin disciplines are affirmations of God's truth about us, prompted by the

Holy Spirit, and profoundly good. Are they needed in you today? I cannot imagine a day without these invaluable "keys" to a prison break from all that would hold us captive. Repent and confess.

One of the most beautiful parts of Nehemiah is the way in which Israel was invited to stand up before the LORD and praise Him, "who is from everlasting to everlasting" (9:5). It does no good to wallow in sin and remain stuck in our failures. It is time to trust in God's compassion and love. Amen.

WEDNESDAY, WEEK THREE

BIBLE INTAKE/MEDITATION

"Do not let this Book of the Law depart from your mouth; meditate on it day and night, so that you may be careful to do everything written in it. Then you will be prosperous and successful." -Joshua 1:8

Most likely when you hear the word "meditation" your mind pulls up an image of someone sitting with their legs crossed, hands on knees with palms facing up, eyes closed, and the continual drone of that familiar humming sound. You may envision people sitting in a circle with leotards on, meditating in a group yoga session. With these images of meditating in mind, you are likely thinking, "no thanks" to the notion of learning this spiritual discipline. Hopefully, today's study will change your mind.

Meditating, according to the Bible, is not an attempt to calm your spirit so that you can reach your center, but instead it is the discipline of quieting your soul so that God's Word can root itself deeply into your heart. Two words from the verse above are of particular importance for our study today. The first is the word translated "law." It is the Hebrew word "tow-rah" (torah) that indicated the first five books of the Old Testament also called the Law of Moses. The second word is the word "meditate." In the original language this word had to do

with moaning, growling, or muttering. To meditate in the Old
Testament meant to make barely audible sounds, like a dog makes
when you approach to take something away from him.

Now, let's look at Joshua's context. What was going on in his life
when God told him to know the Word of God and to meditate on it?
Well, Moses had just died and Joshua had taken his place as leader of
the Israelite nation. Maybe as many as three million people depend-
ed on his leadership and they were positioned on the edge of the
Promised Land ready to take the inheritance God had promised.
Joshua was facing several years of coordinating battles against God's
enemies and assigning land to each of the twelve tribes. This may be
one of the greatest leadership challenges in the Bible. And how did
God say Joshua would be successful? Read the Bible and think about
it all the time!

God told Joshua that the best way for him to lead the people to
their inheritance was to know the Word of God. God did not speak of
provisions for the armies, strategies for winning battles, or instructions for moving the people; these would come later. The most
important thing Joshua could do was to make sure he knew the Word
of God so that he could obey the Word of God and thereby success-
fully live for God. When it comes to spiritual disciplines, taking the
Word of God and meditating on it is equally important for us!

Polls and surveys continue to show that the majority of church goers are "biblically illiterate," despite the overwhelming number of versions, study tools, and Bible study resources. Here's the bottom line: to be a follower of Jesus, to walk in the path of growth, we must work at taking in God's Word, the Bible. Before I give you some suggestions on how to both read and meditate on the Bible, let me give you one encouragement. Don't set your goals too high. We often get overly zealous, set some lofty goals, fail to reach them, get discouraged, and quit. Like going to the gym to workout, learning a new language, or training for a new job; it is best to start small and make progress from there. With that in mind, here are some ways to get the Bible into your heart and mind:

- Commit to reading or listening to the Bible every day. This is simple. Whether it's one verse in bed before you turn the lights out, a Proverb as you're eating breakfast in the morning, some Scripture during a coffee break, or pulling up any number of online resources (like eastviewchurch.net). Ten seconds a day and you're on your way.

- Read a Psalm every day. Using the Jewish hymnbook as your daily guide will allow you to see how the Old Testament people of God communicated with Him and will improve your prayer life as well.

- Read one chapter a day of one of the gospels. Immersing yourself into the life of Christ will help you follow Him better.

- Read 9 chapters a day from the New Testament for a whole month. Doing this will allow you to read the entire New Testament through in one month. If you miss a day, don't sweat it, just go to the next nine chapters for the corresponding day (e.g. if you read Matthew 1-9 on day one, but miss day two, pick up Matthew 19-27 on day three). The same applies if you only read three chapters.

- Buy a journal or Bible that suggests daily verses or selections of Scriptures.

- Read the topical selections from the concordance or special sections in your Bible. Simply look up a word you are interested in like "joy." Find joy in the concordance and then read the corresponding verses.

Okay, that should get you started for Bible intake. But what in the world is meditation and how can I do it? Well, go buy some leotards and sit with your legs crossed...just kidding. Below are a number of ways you can mutter, moan, and growl your way through the Word of God each day.

- Write one of the verses you read on a post-it note or card or someplace you will see it throughout the week. Read it under your breath, muttering it every time you see it throughout the week, allowing it to become part of your thinking.

- Pick a word or phrase from one of the verses you read and memorize that phrase (e.g. "Jesus, said 'follow Me'" or "God loves a cheerful giver"). Repeat it to yourself as you drive, mow the lawn, wash dishes, sit on your deck, watch the kids play baseball or softball, etc... When your spouse or friend catches you mumbling this phrase, you're meditating!

- Find half an hour in a quiet place and read the same verse over and over several times. As you do, a couple of things will happen: you'll probably memorize it and you'll probably begin to really understand it. Close your eyes and think about the words you have now hidden in your heart.

- After one of your Bible readings above pray this prayer: "Father, what from this verse would you like me to really focus on?" Then sit in silence with your eyes closed for five minutes. Don't get discouraged if you don't "hear" God. The Spirit is working on our growth even when we can't feel it.

As far as we know Joshua read his Bible a lot and he meditated on it all through the conquest of Canaan. He won the battles God had for him and we will win our spiritual battles as we do the same.

THURSDAY, WEEK THREE

WITNESS/WORK

"Always be prepared to give an answer to everyone who asks you to give the reason for the hope that you have. But do this with gentleness and respect..." -I Peter 3:15

It's always challenged me that Peter made such a bold assumption here. It's subtle, but Peter assumes that you and I will have people asking us about the hope we possess. He assumes when people observe our lives, not just the spectacular moments, but our normal, day to day lives that it'll spark curiosity and questions. Remember that the mundane, ordinary, common things typically don't spark curiosity in people's lives. So Peter assumes that the way we live and the way we engage in our work will stand out, so much so that we better be prepared to explain why. The gut-wrenching question for us then can only be this: When was the last time someone was so curious about your lifestyle that they stopped to ask you about it?

You see the witness we display and the work we engage in creates space for God. It's in this space, that He spiritually forms us and unleashes His influence on our surroundings. The words translated in this verse "be prepared" come from the Greek word "hetoimos." It's a readiness word that when referring to people could be translated as "preparing to receive the one that's coming." Think about that for a minute! Our life's devotion to following Jesus (personal witness) is preparing us for the one that's coming. That might be someone in your family, a long time friend, or co-worker you never thought in a million years would be seeking God. But they are, you just don't know it and the spiritual disciplines of witness and work put us on the path to intersect them in their search for God. But how do we willingly partner with God to both be transformed and then share that transformation with others? Colossians 3:23 reminds us that:

> "Whatever you do, work at it with all your heart, as working for the Lord, not for men, since you know that you will receive an inheritance from the Lord as a reward."

We willingly partner with God in our work and witness by recognizing His calling for excellence, or holiness in both areas. Pastor and author A.W. Tozer challenged us to consider why we separate the sacred and secular in our lives. The mistaken assumption is that what we do on Sundays is sacred and spiritual. What we do Monday through Saturday is the secular, worldly, routine life. Oh... what would happen in our lives and the lives around us if we'd only realize that God sees no separation? When the sacred and secular come crashing back together in our lives the forces of Hell cannot stop us!

As we reflect on how God transforms others and us through our work and witness let's turn our attention to, of all things, the circus. If you've ever witnessed a performance by Cirque Du Soleil or the

Ringling Brothers and Barnum & Bailey Circus you've seen world-class trapeze artists. Cutting through the air 40 feet above the ground, they catapult themselves, flipping and twisting from one bar to another. They make it look so easy; no doubt the result of years of training. But is there a secret to their success? Theologian and author Henri Nouwen had the opportunity to talk with 'The Flying Rodleighs" who perform in the Simoneit-Barum Circus in Germany. Listen to what they had to say about how they work in tandem to accomplish amazing feats:

> "As a flyer, I must have complete trust in my catcher. The public might think that I am the great star of the trapeze, but the real star is Joe, my catcher. He has to be there for me with split-second precision to grab me out of the air as I come to him in the long jump. The secret is that the flyer does nothing and the catcher does everything. The worst thing a flyer can do is try and catch the catcher. It's Joe's task to catch me. If I grab Joe's wrists, I might break them, or he might break mine, and that would be the end of both of us. When I fly to Joe, I have simply to stretch out my arms and hands and wait for him to catch me and pull me safely up. A flyer must fly, and a catcher much catch, and the flyer must trust, with outstretched arms, that his catcher will be there for him." (Henri Nouwen, *Spiritual Direction,* p. 148-149)

So how does trapeze aerodynamics have anything to do with the spiritual disciplines of witness and work? When we honor God with excellence in our work and witness, it's like we're climbing up the ladder, grabbing the bar, and swinging freely with Him through life. As we swing with Him, we're prepared to receive those who are coming. When that moment comes, we share the hope we have in Christ. We've let go of the safety of the bar. Then, in that weightless moment, we wait for God, the ultimate catcher to safely grab us and the person we've shared with. We've created space for God to shape us spiritually and usher God's Kingdom into someone else's life. It's a beautiful partnership. We voluntarily let go of the bar and God catches us. When we, and many times that other person, arrive on the other bar, God has transformed our lives. We are new creations (II Cor. 5:17). That's a pretty incredible ride.

FRIDAY, WEEK THREE

SILENCE/SOLITUDE

"Very early in the morning, while it was still dark, Jesus got up, left the house and went off to a solitary place, where he prayed."
-Mark 1:35

I think I truly heard it for the first time on top of a mountain ridge somewhere in the backwoods of Big Frog Wilderness in the Cherokee National Park, Southeastern Tennessee. There was a place where the trees opened up and I could see miles and miles of rolling mountains, full and lush with an array of deciduous trees, peppered with evergreens and flowering bushes. I climbed to the highest point on that ridge and sat, totally in awe of the sight, but soon confronted with a sound I was not very familiar with... silence. There were no noises at all. Occasionally I would hear the breeze brush by my ears, but it was silent and I fell in love. God met with me in that silence, filling my heart with the promises of His Scriptures, breathing His peace into my soul, and holding my heavy heart where I no longer felt the weight of life.

It was an experience that I have since repeated often back here in my "real life" of everyday activity and responsibilities. But at that moment on the mountain, I backed into a holy habit that has changed my relationship with God in an immense way. The context of my trip to the mountains that year was a life that was critically imbalanced. I had depleted my reserves of energy in life... relationally, spiritually, and emotionally. I was beginning to redline and with the encouragement of a good boss, and the tenacity of a godly wife, I left almost immediately to retreat to the mountains where I had taken teenagers for years as a youth pastor. My life was too full, and faced with no agenda on that mountain ridge, I entered into a holy silence of my soul, where God finally had my full attention. Alone for seven days in the beauty of the back-country provided a watershed moment for me in regards to silence and solitude, but it's remarkably easy to replicate those moments right back here in everyday life.

Jesus modeled this for us beautifully, as He took time away from a demanding and needy public to be alone with God the Father. He, of all people, would have every excuse in the book to neglect this practice, and yet we see Him value this time. Henri Nouwen, in his book *Out Of Solitude*, writes of Mark 1:35:

> "the more I read this nearly silent sentence locked in between the loud words of action, the more I have the sense that the secret of Jesus is hidden in that lonely place where He went to pray, early in the morning, long before dawn." (p. 13-14)

It appears that Mark intentionally wrapped this verse up in the context of activity. Jesus was doing good stuff here... important stuff. Yet even in this flurry of activity and fame He became recluse... to pray... to center His soul on the One who sent Him. You can't read 1:35 without reading verse 36 where the disciples looked for Jesus and upon finding Him they interrupted His quiet moment and exclaimed "everybody's looking for you!" Yet in a day where the phone is ringing, the text messages and tweets are flying, the kids are banging on the bathroom door, the boss needs you to work late, and you've got to catch up on all your episodes on your DVR, we might dare say that we don't have time for this *luxury*.

Now I don't mean to trivialize your hectic life. You're probably doing a lot of important things... a lot of GOOD things. But that's all the more reason to "come away" with Jesus for silence and solitude... to come to a place where God lifts the pack of burdens off your shoulders and gives you rest in the comfort of His presence. And when you go, don't do all the talking. In good counsel from Solomon and James, go near to listen, be slow to speak, and let your words be few (Ecclesiastes 5:1-2, James 1:19). Gary Moon wrote in his book, *Apprenticeship With Jesus:*

> "In such a transforming friendship [constant, ongoing, interactive friendship] with God, communication includes more than an exchange of words. It advances into deeper communion and consummation." (p. 176)

Quite frankly, in my own experience, silence grows sweeter the more I practice it. It's been an evolving experience for me, where as I mature, it becomes more natural... a far deeper experience than can be captured in words.

I once heard Dallas Willard tell of an interview where Dan Rather, a former CBS newscaster, asked Mother Teresa about praying.

> "When you pray," asked Dan, "what do you say to God?"
> "I don't say anything," she replied. "I listen." Dan replied, "Well, okay... when God speaks to you, then, what does He say?" "He doesn't say anything. He listens." As Dan was caught off guard by the answer, Mother Teresa followed up. "And if you don't understand that," Mother Teresa added, "I can't explain it to you."
> (http://philfoxrose.com/tag/mother-teresa-of-calcutta/)

Solitude and silence brings the opportunity for this type of encounter to take place.

The appendix has a great resource of additional biblical texts, tips for application, and recommended books on this subject. I highly encourage you to read it today.

SATURDAY, WEEK THREE

STEWARDSHIP/SIMPLICITY

**"A man's life does not consist in the abundance
of his possessions." -Luke 12:15**

Abundance is a good thing if it is the right kind of abundance. Jesus said, "I have come to give you abundant life." (John 10:10). Abundance with the spiritual fruit of love, goodness, kindness, joy, etc. leads to a full life. Whereas, abundance in material possessions can lead to destruction. Jesus tells a parable in Luke 12:15-21 to highlight this truth.

> "The ground of a certain rich man produced a good crop. He thought to himself, 'What shall I do? I have no place to store my crops.' Then he said, 'This is what I'll do. I will tear down barns and build bigger ones, and there I will store all my grain and my goods. And I'll say to myself, "You have plenty of good things laid up for many years. Take life easy: eat, drink and be merry."'" "But God said to him, 'You fool! This very night your life will be demanded from you. Then who will get what you have prepared for yourself?' This is how it will be with anyone who stores up things for himself but is not rich towards God."

This parable was told and written over 2,000 years ago. However, this story from Jesus could not be more relevant to us and our culture. It describes the American prosperity mindset: make as much as you can, store up as much as you can, then retire, and live a life of luxury.

Everything we have is a gift from God and is to be used for His glory. (I Chron. 29:14) God does not condemn being rich or having stuff. But God does hold us accountable with the stuff (talents, time, and money) He has given us. One of our God-given roles on this earth is to be a good steward of the stuff He has given us. To be a good steward we need to have an attitude of simplicity or contentment.

One of the ways we can be good stewards is to practice a life of simplicity. The spiritual discipline of simplicity allows our heart, mind, and attitude to be shaped by God into His likeness. This practice places us in a state where we learn to depend on God. Filling our lives with more stuff is rooted in a lack of trust of a God who provides.

> "The inward reality of simplicity involves a life of joyful unconcern for possessions. Neither the greedy nor the miserly know this liberty. It has nothing to do with abundance of possessions or their lack. It is an inward spirit of trust. If what we have we receive as a gift, and if what we have is to be cared for by God, and if what we have is available to others, then we will possess freedom from anxiety. This is the inward reality of simplicity. However, if what we have we believe we have gotten, and if what we have we believe we must hold onto, and if what we have is not available to others, then we live in anxiety. (Richard Foster, *Celebration of Discipline*, p. 87-88)
>
> "God made man simple; man's complex problems are of his own devising." (Ecclesiastes 7:29; JB)

"But godliness with contentment is great gain. For we brought nothing into this world, and we can take nothing out of it. But if we have food and clothing, we will be content with that." (I Timothy 6:6-7)

"I have learned the secret of being content in any and every situation, whether well fed or hungry, whether living in plenty or in want." (Philippians 4:12)

What does a life of simplicity look like? It means living with less, doing fewer activities, being content with what you have, giving yourself and your stuff away to others, and trusting God to provide for your needs (not wants). Try practicing one or more of the following:

- Pick out several of your favorite clothing items in your closet and give them away.
- Loan out your car to a person in need for the week.
- Have your child participate in only one activity or sport this year.
- Make purchases only for their usefulness and not their status.
- Spend the week without using your cell phone.
- Remove all evening appointments and meetings this week along with any technology.
- Go "unplug" and spend face to face time with those you love.
- Set aside a generous amount of money and "bless" another person anonymously.
- Give double what you normally do this Sunday at church.
- Spend time thanking God for what He has given you. Use the alphabet and thank God for something that begins with each letter.
- Pray each morning this week: "Lord, simplify my life so I can be of better use to you today."

The following old Shaker hymn speaks of a life marked by simplicity. Make this hymn your prayer today.

> 'Tis the gift to be simple,
>
>> 'Tis the gift to be free,
>
> 'Tis the gift to come down where you ought to be,
>
> And when we find ourselves in the place just right,
>
>> 'Twill be in the valley of love and delight.
>
> When true simplicity is gained,
>
>> To bow and to bend we shan't be ashamed.
>
> To turn, turn will be our delight
>
>> Till by turning, turning we come round right.

WEEK FOUR
CHANGES US TO LOOK LIKE JESUS

MONDAY

"How great is the love the Father has lavished on us, that we should be called children of God! And that is what we are! The reason the world does not know us is that it did not know him. Dear friends, now we are children of God, and what we will be has not yet been made known. But we know that when he appears, we will be like him, for we shall see him as he is. Everyone who has this hope in him purifies himself, just as he is pure." -1 John 3:1-3

Midnight phone calls rarely bring good news. They are heart-thumping experiences that make me spring out of bed with an instant adrenaline rush and the alertness of a toddler in a church service. Years ago I received a midnight call that I'll never forget. The sniffling and stuttering on the other end of the line gave me pause as I listened carefully for the details of a horrific accident. My best friend labored to share the details of a head-on collision between a mutual friend and a drunk driver, followed with a plea to join him at the hospital where surgeons were frantically working to save Jeff's life.

We arrived at the hospital to greet Jeff's wife and a variety of family and friends. There we eagerly awaited the report from the medical staff. The waiting room became a place of group prayer, anxious silence, and even musical worship as we supported one another through the night. Eventually we received word that Jeff was stable and would be transferred to another hospital by helicopter. Many of us headed for home, relieved by a spared life, but anticipating a long road to recovery.

Phone calls at 6:00 a.m. are greeted differently than the midnight calls. At midnight I am fearful of the news from the other end. At 6:00 a.m. I am frustrated in anticipation of a highly caffeinated morning person with useless trivia. On this particular morning, just a couple of hours after heading home from the hospital, the phone rang again. I expected a cheerful update. What I heard was the same sniffling and stuttering that kicked off this long stretch to daylight. The first coherent statement was "Jimmy, we lost Jeff."

In the next few days we were at the funeral of our good friend and the father of two little boys (2 yrs. old and 2 months old). We searched, as many do, for ways to serve the family and provide support in their need. Our group of friends agreed that one of the most loving things we could do is to write letters to the boys who would never know their father. Each man wrote to Jeff's boys, giving specific details of his character and intricate stories from our encounters with their daddy along the way. Our hope was to leave each boy with a treasure chest of our memories that they could vicariously embrace. While they would certainly grow up to resemble their daddy physically, we longed for them to resemble him in character. We hoped that these letters would be part of a process that helped the boys to be shaped by their father, even in his absence.

More than a dozen years have passed since Jeff's tragic death, but I still reflect on what was and what might be. Today I think of these teenage boys looking in the mirror and seeing a reflection that physically resembles their father. By faith, I smile as I think of how they've grown to be young men of character that love and live like their daddy once did. I trust that these letters are a treasured link between the father and sons.

Each of us has such letters tucked away as well. They are collected between the covers of our Bible and they speak of a loving Father, exemplified in Jesus Christ. These letters stir our hearts and minds about the Father and compel us to resemble the Son. We are called to be Christ-like. Colossians 1:15 notes:

> "He is the image of the invisible God, the firstborn over all creation."

The more we spend time with Him, the more we reveal our family resemblance in Christ. Like Jeff's boys, I read through these notes in hopes of catching a glimpse of the Father. I occasionally look in the mirror in hopes of seeing one who looks more like Jesus today than yesterday.

God has made some incredible promises about our identity and image. He has addressed our past, our present, and our future regarding our transformation to Christlikeness. In short, throughout history and into eternity God calls us to become like Christ. In Romans 8:29 we read:

> "For those God foreknew he also predestined to be conformed to the likeness of his Son..." Foreknowledge and predestination are enormous topics for people of faith. Although there is much to consider here, let's simply acknowledge that God initiated our progress toward Christlikeness.

In our walk, we are also presently being transformed into His likeness. In 2 Corinthians 3:18, Paul addresses the Corinthian church by writing:

> "And we ... are being transformed into his likeness with ever-increasing glory, which comes from the Lord, who is the Spirit."

This is profound news for Christians of every era. We are not simply saved from Hell, but to a family resemblance where we reflect the glory of the Father as followers of the Son, by the power of the Spirit. To use Biblical language, we are provoked beyond mere salvation to ongoing sanctification. This is the "ever-increasing glory" that Paul is describing.

Ultimately, we long for the pinnacle of our *walk* when we will see Him and be like Him. The Apostle John writes:

> "But we know that when he appears, we shall be like him,
> for we shall see him as he is." (1 John 3:2b)

For those who trust in Christ, there will be a day when our faith turns to sight and we are truly changed. I would suggest that a further study of 1 John 3:1-3 would reveal the past, present, and future perspectives of our transformation, all contained in this intriguing passage.

> "How great is the love the Father *has lavished (past perspective)* on us, that we should be called children of God! And *that is what we are (present perspective)*! The reason the world does not know us is that it did not know him. Dear friends, now we are children of God, and what we will be has not yet been made known. But we know that when he appears, *we will be like him (future perspective)*, for we shall see him as he is. Everyone who has this hope in him purifies himself, just as he is pure." (1 John 3:1-3; emphasis mine)

As we have been learning, *God the Holy Spirit takes the initiative* in our lives. He does so through *various means, in cooperation with our response.* The pressing question of this chapter is, "Are you looking like Jesus?" I'm not suggesting your grow a beard and wear sandals. I am asking you if your character is being transformed into that of Christ. Jesus has called us to follow Him, but His ways are countercultural. His claims are incredible, and the expectation is that our identity is hidden in His (Col. 3:3). To state the obvious, this requires change.

> "The process of being conformed to the image of Christ takes place primarily at the points of our unlikeness to Christ's image. God is present to us in the most destructive aspects of our cultural captivity. God is involved with us in the most imprisoning bondage of our brokenness. God meets us in those places of our lives that are most alienated from God. God is there, in grace, offering us the forgiveness, the cleansing, the liberation, the healing we need to begin the journey toward our wholeness and fulfillment in Christ." (M. Robert Mulholland, Jr. *Invitation to a Journey,* p. 37)

We would prefer to *reveal* the parts of our lives that are aligned with Christ and *conceal* the areas that are in opposition to Christ's reign. But that is not transformation, but a cheap cover up. Let me say it differently. If we are as serious about Christlikeness as God is, we all have some work to do. We need to be honest about the areas of our lives that have yet to be surrendered to His Lordship. It is in those areas that Jesus longs to meet us and empower us to look more like Himself. There is more to be done and there is more to become!

The remainder of this chapter is dedicated to studying some of the most memorable and foundational teachings of Christ. The "Beatitudes" that Jesus taught His followers demonstrate the depth of His wisdom and the vast distinction between His Kingdom reign and the culture of today. Philip Yancey notes:

> "In a life characterized by poverty, mourning, meekness, a hunger for righteousness, mercy, purity, peacemaking, and persecution, Jesus himself embodied the Beatitudes." (Philip Yancey, *The Jesus I Never Knew,* p. 126)

In Matthew 5:3-12 Jesus says:

> "Blessed are the poor in spirit, for theirs is the kingdom of heaven. Blessed are those who mourn, for they will be comforted. Blessed are the meek, for they will inherit the earth. Blessed are those who hunger and thirst for righteousness, for they will be filled. Blessed are the merciful, for they will be shown mercy. Blessed are the pure in heart, for they will see God. Blessed are the peacemakers, for they will be called children of God. Blessed are those who are persecuted because of righteousness, for theirs is the kingdom of heaven. Blessed are you when people insult you, persecute you and falsely say all kinds of evil against you because of me. Rejoice and be glad, because great is your reward in heaven, for in the same way they persecuted the prophets who were before you."

A fitting foreword to the next five daily devotionals has been mined from Dallas Willard's book *The Divine Conspiracy*. There he stirs the would-be readers of the Beatitudes by saying:

> "We can savor them, affirm them, meditate upon them, and

engrave them on plaques to hang on our walls. But a major question remains: How are we to *live* in response to them? … It will help us to know what to do – and what not to do – with the Beatitudes if we can discover what Jesus himself was doing with them." (p. 98)

May God richly bless you as you journey through the rest of this chapter and apply the modeling and teaching of Christ into your own walk.

DAILY READING: "the Beatitudes"

• Changes Us to Look Like Jesus	Monday
• Blessed are the poor (Matthew 5:3)	Tuesday
• Blessed are those who mourn (Matthew 5:4)	Wednesday
• Blessed are the meek (Matthew 5:5)	Thursday
• Blessed are those who hunger and thirst (Matthew 5:6)	Friday
• Blessed are those who are merciful (Matthew 5:7)	Saturday

TUESDAY, WEEK FOUR

BLESSED ARE THE POOR IN SPIRIT

"Blessed are the poor in Spirit, for theirs is the kingdom of heaven." -Matthew 5:3 "For he has not despised or disdained the suffering of the afflicted one; he has not hidden his face from him but has listened to his cry for help" -Psalm 22:24

The Old Testament people of God had a notion that wealth, prosperity, children, and victory over enemies signified His blessing on one's life. Of course, God did bless His original covenant people with physical blessings. He made Abraham the father of many nations. He gave Solomon great wealth. He caused David to triumph over all of his enemies for forty years as king. He made Jacob prosper by multiplying his share of the herds and flocks he tended for his uncle Laban. So, the people of God found it easy to label blessed and "unblessed" people simply by noting their outward success.

You can see this attitude expressed by the disciples of Jesus' question concerning the blind man.

"Rabbi, who committed the sin that caused him to be born blind, this man or his parents?" (John 9:2)

Since the blind man suffered this physical malady, it was an obvious sign to the early followers of Christ that he was a sinner and therefore, not blessed. This attitude prevailed from the time of

Abraham to the time of Jesus' ministry on earth and led to a spiritual elitism among those who were prosperous and judgment of those who were not. Those who were rich and successful were definitely kingdom people and those who were not were on the outside looking in. In one sermon, Jesus changed every kingdom-of-God perception. Nine times in this sermon on the mountain Jesus defines those who are truly blessed and dispelled this judgmental thinking.

First of all, let's define "blessing." Blessing is divine favor from God. The first century followers understood blessing as a deep-down spiritual joy that came from knowing one had a place in the kingdom of God. God's favor signified belonging, thus one had a joyful outlook based on God's acceptance. You can see why the poor would feel like they had no place in the grand plan of God in the world. But Jesus came along and gave these simple followers a new understanding of blessing. According to Him the economy of blessing was about to change. He did NOT say, "blessed are the wealthy, prosperous and victorious." Instead, He blessed attitudes of the heart and soul. He began with the poor in spirit.

What exactly does it mean to be "poor" in spirit? Well, the word translated poor here is a word that means to beg. It came from a root word that meant "to crouch." So the word poor is exactly what we think it is. The picture is of someone who is lacking money, food, or shelter driven to take lowly positions in the public square, sitting at the side of the road, begging for alms. If you ever visit a large city, you have likely encountered several homeless people shaking a cup or can hoping for some change. There is a sad humility one must have to take this position. Often, they will not offer eye contact for shame.

Jesus says that if we want favor from God, then we must have this same kind of humble attitude spiritually speaking. What would cause us to take such a humble spiritual stance? It would be a deep realization of our poverty of righteousness before God. If you and I could see our spiritual lives through God's eyes, we would see how beggarly, how unworthy, and how desperately poor we are before the perfection of His eternal greatness. In turn, we would simply "crouch" before Him and beg for mercy. In the kingdom of God, Jesus says the blessed ones are the ones who realize how unworthy they are and bow before God in humility. In fact, he promises that these "poor in spirit" souls are in the kingdom of heaven right now!

Jesus would later tell a parable about a Pharisee and a tax collector praying which illustrates this kingdom principle. The Pharisee was blessed by outward appearances and prayed a confident prayer of entitlement to the kingdom. He was "confident of [his] own righteousness and looked down on everybody else." (Luke 18:9) He prayed:

"God, I thank you that I am not like other men - robbers, adulterers - or even like this tax collector..." (Luke 18:11)

He was sure he was blessed and part of the kingdom. The tax collector on the other hand,

"...stood at a distance...would not even look up to heaven, but beat his breast and said, 'God, have mercy on me, a sinner.'" (Luke 18:13)

He was sure that he was not worthy of blessing or of being part of God's kingdom.

Both the Pharisee and tax collector were wrong in their assumptions. The blessed in the kingdom are those who humbly understand their spiritual poverty before God and beg for forgiveness. Those who think they are entitled to God's love because of their success are not blessed and are not a part of the kingdom. Which attitude reflects your heart today?

WEDNESDAY, WEEK FOUR

BLESSED ARE THOSE WHO MOURN

"Blessed are those who mourn, for they will be comforted" -
Matthew 5:4

I was a young married preacher serving a small rural congregation. The parsonage phone rang. We shared a "party line" and if you
don't know what that means just remember there was a time when
cell phones and computers didn't exist. I knew the peculiar ring tone
for our phone, so I answered. It was the local funeral home director.
One of the teenagers in that country church had just taken his own
life and his parents, faithful members, were waiting for me to help
them make the arrangements. I had never made a pastoral visit on a
grieving family, but off I went with a car load of anxiousness and a
heart full of heaviness. Fortunately for me a very seasoned elder, and
one of my professors at Lincoln Christian Seminary, had already
arrived. We sat in his car for a few minutes in order to pray and prepare to talk with the family. I don't recall all that we said or did in the
next thirty minutes, but I do remember the grief and the tears – theirs
and ours. I can't imagine walking into that home and offering
Matthew 5:4 as a word of comfort. Strangely, Jesus did that very
thing to those who experienced life's broken heart.

"Blessed are those who mourn," He said. Weird. In effect, Jesus was saying, "Congratulations when you feel the terrible loss of the one you love." Odd - I might even say, "That's inappropriate." The word Jesus chose was not difficult to translate or understand. "Pentheo" was commonly used of mourning for the dead, of expressing sorrow or grief over a loved one's departure from this life to the next one. It is the kind of grief you can't hold inside. It's the sort of mourning that must be released. It's used ten times in the New Testament in a variety of ways. It wouldn't take long to get a feel for how the various writers incorporate it (See Matthew 9:15; Luke 6:25; 1 Corinthians 5:2; 2 Corinthians 12:11; James 4:9; Revelation 18:11; 18:15; 18:19; and Mark 16:10). A couple of examples might help. Mark 16:10 describes how the disciples were feeling over the arrest and crucifixion of Jesus. They were weeping and mourning. 1 Corinthians 5:2 tells us someone in the life of the First Christian Church in Corinth, Greece was committing sexual sin and didn't even feel one ounce of mourning. Paul, their church planter and disciple of Jesus, couldn't comprehend that kind of arrogance and he told them so. One final example from Paul will suffice, same church, months later. He was now afraid that when he came to Corinth for a pastoral visit he would be the only one grieved "over many who have sinned earlier and have not repented of the impurity, sexual sin and debauchery in which they have indulged."

So, how does this particular beatitude play a part in changing us to look like Jesus? We know that Jesus mourned over loss. He never denied its existence. He was deeply moved, troubled, and wept at the death of his dear friend, Lazarus (John 11:33-35). Jesus also expressed similar feelings when He approached the city of Jerusalem for the last time and took a moment to reflect on her future. The Bible tells us He broke down and cried (Luke 19:41). Let's clear the air. Jesus was not being hard-hearted or making light of real personal pain when He announced on that Galilean mountainside, "Blessed are those who mourn." Rather, He was saying the values of the Kingdom differ sharply from those of the world. The world considers people blessed who win the lottery, associate with the "beautiful people," or find happiness in shallow experiences. In contrast, it is the person who hungers for more, is not satisfied with the glitter and sparkle of the world's trinkets that ultimately finds real encouragement and genuine comfort in what only God can give.

The day of the funeral arrived for that family I mentioned at the start of this devotional. Mourning filled everything and everyone, including me. I can still hear the sounds of family and friends grieving. I couldn't even finish the sermon. Their grief became my grief. Eventually, I prayed. All of us drove to the cemetery. Some words were said. I prayed again. We got back in our cars and drove to the church building for a meal. Comfort was what was served that day. Those people knew how to love one another. I watched and learned how Kingdom mourners can look like Jesus and become more and more like Jesus. That small congregation exemplified what it was like to "feel you've lost what is most dear to you. Only then can you be embraced by the One most dear to you." (*The Message*) It is in that moment and moments just like it when God changes us to look more and more like Jesus. What a paradox.

Thursday, Week Four

BLESSED ARE THE MEEK

"Blessed are the meek, for they will inherit the earth."
-Matthew 5:5

If you were within earshot of Jesus when He was talking, you were listening. Whether you loved Him, hated Him, or were confused by Him, you were listening. His teaching and ways were so counter-cultural you never knew what He was about to say. In the beatitudes we hear Jesus tell his followers "blessed are the meek, for they will inherit the earth." In Jesus' time, classic Greek culture profoundly impacted the Roman Empire worldview. Meekness wasn't viewed as a virtue but a vice. People viewed meekness as being beneath, or sub-servient to someone or something. Jesus operated in a culture that val-ued success, prestige, wealth, and power. Sound familiar?

Yet, Jesus tells us plainly that the meek will inherit the earth. Meekness, sometimes described as gentleness, produces the fruit of self-control. It's not a term we're familiar with. Meekness is the hum-ble dependence on God to work in and through us. To be meek, is to be utterly dependent on God, a voluntary submission to the ways and will of God. In *A Praying Life,* Paul Miller notes:

> "The great struggle of my life is not trying to discern God's will; it is trying to discern and then disown my own." (p. 157)

To be meek is to trust in God, commit your ways to Him, and live in a state of quietness before the Lord.

Perhaps a quick example might stir our hearts. In Exodus 14 we find the Israelites in a terribly vulnerable position. Stuck between the Red Sea and the advancing Egyptian Army they wait for the inevitable. If the Egyptians reached them, the Israelites face murder, rape, and kidnapping. In the face of crises, reflect on the words of Moses, a leader who personified meekness:

> "Do not be afraid. Stand firm and you will see the deliverance the Lord will bring today. The Egyptians you see today you will never see again. The Lord will fight for you; you need only to be still." Exodus 14:13-14

Meekness doesn't imply weakness or passive inactivity. Pharaoh certainly didn't view Moses as weak, inactive, or ineffective. Meekness means committing our cause to God and not needing to defend ourselves. Moses commands the Israelites to be still, turn their current situation over to God, and allow Him to work. As they wait on the Lord, His power is unleashed. The meek view their current circumstance through the eternal story God's weaving all around them.

According to Jesus, the meek inherit the earth, not the aggressive, assertive, or manipulative. That seems to fall short in a world that rewards those that claw their way to the top. Again, turning to scripture, we see the Israelites closest to the promise land when most vulnerable to life's circumstances. When we embrace our dependence on God and detect His movements in our daily lives we become more like Jesus, who is "gentle and humble in heart" (Matthew 11:29).

Meekness is the opposite of manipulation, trying to assert our will, and manipulate God's for personal gain. Sadly, we re-visit the Israelites' journey to the promised land to see this play out:

> "So the Philistines fought, and the Israelites were defeated and every man fled to his tent. The slaughter was very great; Israel lost thirty thousand foot soldiers. The ark of God was captured, and Eli's two sons, Hophni and Phinehas, died." I Samuel 4:10-11

Here, the enemy not only gets to them but also slaughters them. Worse than that, the Philistines rode off with Israel's most prized possession... the Ark of the Covenant. In the first story, the Lord fights for His people. In the second, the Philistines slaughter them by the thousands. In the first story, Moses told the Israelites to be still. Against the Philistines, every man "fled to his tent." Moses promised deliverance from the Egyptians and the Philistines brought physical and spiritual destruction. So what happened? The spiritual leaders of Israel lost any sense of meekness. Instead of depending on God they did what they saw fit. Though they were far from God, when life got tough, they tried to manipulate God. Without God's prompting, they brought the Ark of the Covenant into battle, waving it around like a magic wand. An absence of meekness and obedience lost the battle that day, not the absence or presence of the Ark.

Meekness changes us to look more like Christ. We too exclaim, "It is finished," as we die to earthly desires, a need to defend ourselves, to have the last word, to be in control, to cling to security, and predictability and ultimately this allows God to usher in His power and Kingdom. Meekness unleashes the power of the living God in our lives.

FRIDAY, WEEK FOUR

BLESSED ARE THOSE WHO HUNGER AND THIRST

"Blessed are those who hunger and thirst for righteousness, for they will be filled." -Matthew 5:6

Working with children has given me an avenue back into the honest and raw questions of a child-like faith. Sometimes things get complicated the more we play with it. Like a good batch of flapjacks, you don't want to be messin' with the batter too much, or you'll ruin 'em. Likewise, some of the beauty of a simple truth can turn ugly when the theological boxing gloves come on. Sometimes all that's left is confusion, frustration, stubborn opinions, and a lost-but-important matter of faith that the everyday student doesn't know what to do with anymore. I think our beatitude for today fits in that discussion.

Speaking of children, their questions can often point to simple but important things that I frankly haven't thought about for a while. Sometimes they have funny questions like "If God doesn't like mean people, why did He make my big sister?" Or, "Did they really talk that fancy in the Bible Times?" But they ask deep questions too like "If God made everything, then who made God?" And of course your smart alecks go for the tried and true stumpers like "If God can do anything, can He make a rock He can't move?" But there is a question that we often get that points to our beatitude for today. They'll ask, "If Jesus never sinned, why did He get baptized?"

Well John the Baptist had the same objection, but Jesus' response teaches us something important. Jesus replied, "I must do this to fulfill all righteousness." You see, living a God-honoring life is not just about "not doing anything wrong," but it's also about doing things right. The Greek word for righteousness in Matthew's account of Jesus' baptism in 4:15 is the same word for righteousness in our beatitude for today in Matthew 5:6. But righteousness is one of those things that you think you know what it is until you have to explain it to a 5 year old. Then you have to go simple and talk about doing right... being the person God meant for you to be... thinking, feeling, and behaving right. But it's in this simple explanation of a word that I have found great fodder for meditation. Keeping in step with the scope of this series, we see how God the Holy Spirit takes the initiative through various means in cooperation with our response to change us to look like Jesus. Jesus was righteous on His own. We are made righteous by Jesus' sacrifice. So herein lies the question... shall we go on sinning that His grace can increase? By no means! ABSOLUTELY NOT! (Romans 6:1-2) Out of a righteousness given to us by God, we pursue righteousness as a virtue that marks a Jesus follower. We pursue it like a hungry lion in full sprint after its prey

(1st Timothy 6:11) or a thirsty wild animal in search of water (Psalm 42:1). We pursue the integrity, purity, and virtue that define a righteous person.

Let's turn to the rest of the verse… "hunger and thirst… shall be filled." We all eat and drink, therefore, we understand the imagery here. Hunger and thirst refer to desire. Hunger happens in the absence of food; thirst in the absence of drink. It's the desire that Jesus is talking about – not the accomplishment. Remember that in His Jewish audience there were many people who had confused what righteous living was all about. They knew how to act, talk, and look, but their hearts were far from God (Matthew 15:8). You might consider the fact that Jesus speaks of this after explaining the three chief expressions of a right relationship with God (of personal piety), in the first century Jewish culture – giving, praying, and fasting in Matthew 6:1ff. When we show off our own righteousness, God does not show up with His righteousness. Jesus is pointing toward heart language. Far be it from Jesus to load us down with the burden of perfect living. It's the desire to live right that Jesus calls us to. … and not just "kinda" want to do the right thing. Otherwise His beatitude might read more like "Blessed are those who wish they would do the right thing most of the time. For sometimes they'll get it right and sometimes they won't."

Jesus wants to see a deep-seated desire to live the lives we were intended to live. Jesus hungered to do everything right, from His baptism to His crucifixion; it was God's will that mattered most. French mathematician and physicist, Blaise Pascal in the height of the Enlightenment... in the age of the mind... said something very important about the HEART behind this beatitude:

"We do not weary of eating and sleeping every day, for hunger and sleepiness recur. Without that we should weary of them. So, without the hunger for spiritual things, we weary of them." (p. 206-207)

If you see a formulaic life being called for in Matthew 5:6, you miss the heart of it all. It's the same reason Jesus was baptized... you have to DEEPLY WANT to do the right thing. Congratulations to anyone who is starving for God. He will give Himself in abundance. He is the one who makes everything right, including you and me.

SATURDAY, WEEK FOUR

BLESSED ARE THE MERCIFUL

"Blessed are those who are merciful." -Matthew 5:7

God's mercy, grace, and patience often are seen together in Scripture. They are all extensions of God's goodness. God's mercy can be defined as His goodness toward those in misery and distress. God's grace can be defined as His goodness toward those who deserve only punishment. (One way to remember this is by the acronym G.R.A.C.E. which means: God's Riches At Christ's Expense.) God's patience can be defined as His goodness in withholding of punishment toward those who sin.

The word "mercy" is recorded 129 times in the Bible (NIV). A helpful exercise is to go to a website like www.blueletterbible.org and type the word "mercy" into the search tab. Then read through and meditate on the verses. There is a sample below. If we want to be like Jesus then we must show mercy to others because that is what He has shown to us.

> "The Lord has heard my cry for mercy; the Lord accepts my prayer." Psalm 6:9

> "Do not withhold your mercy from me, O Lord; may your love and your truth always protect me." Psalm 40:11

> "Have mercy on me, O God, have mercy on me, for in you my soul takes refuge. I will take refuge in the shadow of your wings until the disaster has passed." Psalm 57:1

"Answer me, O Lord, out of the goodness of your love; in your great mercy turn to me." Psalm 69:16

"Have mercy on me, O Lord, for I call to you all day long. Hear my prayer, O LORD; listen to my cry for mercy." Psalm 86:3, 6

"The Lord is merciful and gracious; slow to anger and abounding in steadfast love." Psalm 103:8

"I love the Lord, for he heard my voice; he heard my cry for mercy." Psalm 116:1

"We do not make requests of you because we are righteous, but because of your great mercy." Daniel 9:18b

"He has showed you, O man, what is good. And what does the LORD require of you? To act justly and to love mercy and to walk humbly with your God." Micah 6:8

"Who is a God like you, who pardons sin and forgives . . . you do not stay angry forever but delight to show mercy." Micah 7:18

"But because of his great love for us, God who is rich in mercy, made us alive with Christ even when we were dead in transgressions." Ephesians 2:4-5

"Let us then approach the throne of grace with confidence, so that we may receive mercy and find grace in our time of need." Hebrews 4:16

Keep these in mind as you reflect on a story of mercy from the book of Luke.

Bartimaeus, a blind man, was begging by the road side leading into Jericho when Jesus, the disciples, and a large crowd passed by him. When the man heard it was Jesus passing by he began to shout *"Jesus, Son of David, have mercy on me."* Many rebuked him and told him to be quiet but he shouted all the more, *"Have mercy on me!"* So Jesus stopped, called the man to draw near, and said to him, "Receive your sight; your faith has healed you." Immediately, he received his sight and followed Jesus, praising God. (Mark 10:46-52; Luke 18:35-42)

Bartimaeus was in desperate need. He was blind, poor, marginalized, and had to beg to survive. He knew his condition and knew he needed mercy. The crowd and the disciples who were with Jesus not only tried to ignore the man who needed help but when he cried out for mercy they rebuked him and told him to be quiet! Jesus on the other hand had compassion and was compelled to grant the man's repeated and heartfelt cry for mercy. He asked the man who was far off to draw near (don't miss this point) and then gave mercy by healing him physically and spiritually.

Who are you like? Maybe you are like the disciples. You spend time with Jesus, learn from Him, talk about Him, but show little or no mercy to those in need. In which case how can you show mercy to those around you today? Maybe you are like Bartimaeus and are in desperate need of mercy today. In which case, ask God for His mercy! Make the following spiritual song your closing prayer for today.

The Church

Verse 1

We are the change

The world is waiting for

We've got a love

The world is desperate for

We will lead

And take to Your streets

Chorus

Now's the time for us to rise

And carry hope

And let love shine

And show the world

That mercy is alive

Now's the time for us to rise

And carry hope

To hopeless eyes

And show this world

That mercy is alive

Verse 2

We're not afraid

We will abandon all

To hear Your name

On lips across the world

We will run

In the wake of Your love

Repeat Chorus

Bridge 1

Fill our hearts

With Your compassion

Let our love be active here

Fill our hearts

With Your compassion

Let our love be real

Be real

Repeat Chorus

Tag

We will go

Where You tell us to go

We will speak out

Your very word

We will move

When You tell us to move

We are Yours

We are Yours

Written by Chris Brown | Mack Brock

© 2010 Elevation Worship Publishing

WEEK FIVE

IN ORDER TO SERVE OTHERS

MONDAY

"Egotism is one of the repulsive manifestations of pride. It is the practice of thinking and speaking much of oneself, the habit of magnifying one's attainments or importance. It leads one to consider everything in its relation to himself rather than in relation to God and the welfare of His people."
-J. Oswald Sanders, *Spiritual Leadership*

"What did you think of the service on Sunday?" Be careful, the question admittedly is a set up. The truth is that I ask that question of people from time to time when I'm feeling ornery. It is usually a way for me to provoke volunteer leaders to consider the lens through which they view church services. Think about how you would respond to that question regarding last Sunday's service. Would you reflect on musical preferences or your ability to relate to the sermon? Would you comment on the way you felt as you were walking out the door? Would you think about the way in which you served?

In our earlier years of following Christ we might be prone to think of the "service" as something to attend with the mindset of a consumer. Then the value of the "service" was directly related to the benefits received. As we mature, we attend with the mindset of a servant. I suppose it is a bit like Christmas. Opening gifts used to be interesting as long as I was the one opening them! I couldn't understand how the adults could hide their disappointment in receiving so few gifts. Now I understand. I'm more interested in those opening the gifts I've given. My frame of reference has been completely altered regarding gift exchanges.

In a similar way, the service is less about what we personally receive, but what we personally contribute to the fellowship of believers. And this goes far beyond Sunday mornings. This is the vantage point by which we view our small groups, our families, our marriages, and our lives. In short, we are being *changed to look like Jesus ... in order to serve others.*

Every gift we are given is for the sake of others. God has brilliantly designed the "body" (church) to function in collaboration with one another. We are members of one another (Romans 12:5) and we have particular areas where we were designed to serve for the sake of the body. Our faith is not to be lived out in isolation, but in community. Remarkably, God has arranged us to serve one another in humility rather than to clamor for positions of prestige or power. In fact, His Kingdom is advanced through service and sacrifice. His way, in stark contrast to the way of our culture, is one of submission.

In his book *The Jesus Way*, Eugene Peterson notes:

"God's way, always, is to use servants. Servants: men and women without standing, without accomplishment, without influence. The core element in a servant identity is *not* being God, not being in charge, not taking the initiative. Or, to put it positively, a servant enters into what has already been decided by another, what is already going on, alert to the gestures and guidance of the Master (Ps. 123). The servant doesn't know the whole story, doesn't know the end from the beginning. The servant's task is to be competent in the immediate affairs that have to do with what he knows of the desires of his Master. All the while he is also aware that there is far more going on, both good and evil, than he has any knowledge of. He lives, in other words, in a mystery but not in confusion." (p. 174)

When we embrace the role of a servant, we demonstrate our understanding that the most important agenda is not our own, but God's. Our service to others demonstrates the surrender of our will to His.

Henri Nouwen helped me to understand this idea of service a bit better in his book *Spiritual Direction*. In this book, Nouwen wrote of "downward mobility" and "voluntary displacement." Downward mobility describes the counter-cultural way of Jesus that prompts us to choose the least comfortable seat in the room, the end of the line, and to pass on the closest parking space. While our society demands that we pursue upward mobility (career advancement, publicity, notoriety, etc.), our Lord quietly models a different course. Downward mobility is ultimately seen in our Savior's descent from heaven to the manger, from the throne of heaven to the cross of Golgotha.

Voluntary displacement causes the hopes and dreams of self to be crowded out by the commission of Christ. The couple that displaces a resort in the Bahamas for a building project in Haiti understands voluntary displacement. The man who sacrifices an hour of sleep so that he can meet for a Bible study knows the impact of voluntary displacement. The woman who turns off the TV and prays with her children at night recognizes voluntary displacement. Our Lord's life and death demonstrate the displacing of His own will in order to submit to the will of the Father (Matt. 26:39).

What we are talking about is serving one another as both a command and by-product stemming from our relationship with Jesus. The more we become like Him, the more we will serve others. In the coming daily readings we will take a closer look at what Jesus has taught and modeled regarding service. We will study the disciples' misunderstandings about serving, Jesus' vivid service to the disciples and the world, and His reinstatement of a disoriented disciple to ongoing service.

Here's a quick look at the daily devotionals to come:

Monday: ... in order to serve others ...

Tuesday: What do you want me to do for you? Mark 10:35-45

Wednesday: Who is the greatest?   Mark 9:33-37

Thursday: Are you going to wash my feet?   John 13:1-17

Friday: Why have you forsaken me?   Matthew 27:45-54

Saturday: Do you love me?   John 21:1-19

Before we wrap up this discussion I'd like to take us to a section of Scripture that captures the essence of Jesus in a powerful and concise passage. It is first shared in Isaiah 42 and then quoted in Matthew. Take a moment to carefully read this potent prophecy and fulfillment from Matthew 12:18-21:

"Here is my servant whom I have chosen,
   the one I love, in whom I delight;
I will put my Spirit on him,
   and he will proclaim justice to the nations.
He will not quarrel or cry out;
   no one will hear his voice in the streets.
A bruised reed he will not break,
   and a smoldering wick he will not snuff out,
   till he leads justice to victory.
In his name the nations will put their hope."

What a powerful segment of Scripture! In these few verses we can see that God's plan was to send a servant (Jesus) to usher in a new kind of kingdom. The original text is a prophetic proclamation in Isaiah 42 (written about 700 years before the birth of Christ). John remembered this Old Testament text as he wrote the Gospel of John, pointing to Jesus as the "servant" whom the prophet spoke of so long ago. Servant leadership was always the plan and priority of the Father.

A closer look at this passage reveals two other qualities of Jesus that seem incompatible. We read that He will "proclaim justice to the nations" and that "in his name the nations will put their hope." This Servant is about justice and hope for the nations! This is not an insignificant little band of brainwashed believers. This is a world-altering campaign that changes the course of history! The scope of this Servant's influence is global and eternal.

Yet, there is tenderness that characterizes this Servant. Although He has a global impact, He did not promote Himself. There was no public relations firm helping Him to campaign for office. In fact, I would suggest that while He relentlessly defended the Father, He grew silent when circumstances called for Him to defend Himself. Perhaps there is something for us to learn in this example!

Finally, He tenderly cares for the "bruised reed" and the "smoldering wick." This is good news for those who feel that they are "bruised" or running out of wax! His servant leadership is one of mending and fanning into flame rather than breaking and snuffing out. When we accurately assess the character of Christ, we run to Him in time of weakness rather than hide from Him. He is a tender warrior, upholding and defending the weak!

What does this mean for us? As we continue to examine what it means to *walk*, let us consider His example of service. We want to look more and more like Jesus and that compels us to serve as Jesus served. He is for justice. He offers hope. He doesn't promote Himself. He mends the broken. He stokes the fire in others. That is servanthood. That is our Savior. That is the path we are to *walk*.

Tuesday, Week Five

What do you want me to do for you?

"Then James and John, the sons of Zebedee, came to Him. 'Teacher,' they said, 'we want you to do for us whatever we ask.' 'What do you want me to do for you?' He asked. They replied, 'Let one of us sit at your right and the other at your left in your glory.' 'You don't know what you are asking,' Jesus said ...When the ten heard about this, they became indignant with James and John...Jesus called them together and said... 'Whoever wants to be first must be slave of all. For even the Son of Man did not come to be served, but to serve, and to give His life as a ransom for many.'" -Mark 10:35-45

I've never met anyone who didn't have at least one blind spot in their life. There is a point in all of us where we fail to see things clearly, especially as it relates to real Christian service, the kind that nourishes spiritual growth. Believe it or not, I once came home from a long day of ministry to find the house in complete disarray, a super-sized-mess. My wife was sitting calmly at the kitchen table while our two pre-school age children were playing in the piles of debris. I had the audacity to ask, "What in the world has happened here today?" If looks could kill I would have been dead on the spot. My wife didn't need to say a word. I caught the message loud and clear. "How would you like to cook meals, change diapers, and care for a one and four year old all day? If you want to clean the house, be my guest!" I quickly changed the subject with, "Ok. I think McDonald's sounds good right now." When brothers, James and John, asked for the moon

from Jesus they had no idea what they were truly saying. Blind spots

are like that. Let's capture the context.

Jesus has been preaching, teaching, and healing in southern

Palestine, east of the Jordan, in Herod Antipas' backyard, a place

called Perea (See Mark 10:1). He's been bombarded with questions,

challenged about His authority, and required to deal with ministry

issues (10:2; 10:13; 10:17; 10:46; and 11:3). The literary context

includes six stories all compacted into a solitary narrative from Mark

10:1 through 11:11. Every place we turn as readers we encounter

another blind spot. The Pharisees had a blind spot to the creation

story and failed to understand marriage and divorce (10:1-12). Jesus'

own disciples had a blind spot to children and the nature of the

Kingdom (10:13-16). The "rich young man" who encountered Jesus

"on His way" had a blind spot to his own great wealth and what it

meant to live in a loving relationship with God (10:17-31). Jump

ahead in the larger context and notice with me that the Jericho folks

and the twelve disciples had a blind spot to compassion when it came

to blind Bartimaeus (10:46-52). What an irony! Last of all, the

Jerusalem crowd portrayed a blind spot to Jesus' true identity as they

whooped and hollered for Him at His "triumphal entry" to the city

(11:1-11). They were looking for a strong military conqueror and an astute politician to lead them out from under Roman dominance. This Messiah is not like that. I think you get the point. All of us are capable of crippling blind spots. Now back to James and John.

Jesus had predicted on three separate occasions His death, burial, and resurrection (Mark 8:31; 9:31 and here). In Mark 10:32-34 He offered His final prediction. The twelve did not grasp what Jesus was saying. The reason I know this is found in the request of James and John. Jesus had been talking about pain and the brothers want to talk about prominence. Jesus had been sharing about suffering and the boys want to chat about supremacy. Jesus had been inviting them into a life of humble service and these two have been elevating haughty "self-hood." Mark, the Gospel writer, is brutally honest. He says the other ten disciples were "indignant" (10:41). It means they were boiling hot, passionately angry, and greatly grieved. Perhaps that word "indignant" revealed their true heart. Maybe they were heated because they had not thought of asking for center-stage in the unfolding story of the Kingdom first. Jesus called the group together for a holy huddle. One more time, He reminded them of the nature of the Kingdom and the life of a radical servant. Please don't miss it. If we want to look like Jesus we are invited to love like Jesus. If we want to think like Jesus we are invited to trust like Jesus. If we want to stand like Jesus we are invited to serve like Jesus. There is no easy way. Jesus' question (the same one He asked Bartimaeus in 10:51) is the just-right-question for us today. "What do you want me to do for you?" Could we dare answer with the Jesus-kind-of-humility? "Please, Lord, make me a servant like you." If so, our walk with Him, our growing to look like Him, and our need for His healing of our blind spots is in very safe hands. Those who serve tend to soar and those who don't tend to sulk.

WEDNESDAY, WEEK FIVE

WHO IS THE GREATEST?

"Sitting down, Jesus called the Twelve and said, 'If anyone wants
to be first, he must be the very last, and the servant of all'"
-Mark 9:35
"Not so with you. Instead, whoever wants to be great among you
must be your servant, and whoever wants to be first
must be slave of all." -Mark 10:43-44

Okay, is anyone paying attention here? Apparently, Jesus' closest followers were missing His point! In these two verses for the day Jesus is stating in plain terms what should be quite obvious to these guys by now. The first verse comes as a result of the guys arguing about who was the greatest among them and the second follows a request made by James and John for places of honor in Jesus' kingdom. These followers were missing two points based on the context of the ministry of which they were a part.

MISSED POINT NUMBER ONE - Jesus is great.

There is no excuse for Peter, James, and John. They had been invited to the top of a mountain with Jesus and witnessed Him in full spiritual glory. Not to mention they saw the most famous guys from the Old Testament, Moses and Elijah! In the presence of such greatness, the Father exalted Jesus above them all (see Mark 9:1-7). How could John and James later come to Jesus and ask to be the number one and two guys in His kingdom (Mark 10:35-37)? How could Peter be a part of any discussion which claimed greatness on his own part? Did they think they were greater than the Old Testament legends? What these three witnessed on the mountain was the eternal greatness of Jesus (and should have helped them see their lack of greatness).

Meanwhile back down the mountain, the other nine disciples were struggling with a demon possessed boy. They were no match for the demon but when Jesus came onto the scene, the demon left as Jesus commanded the spirit never to return (Mark 9:25). Jesus is so great the spiritual realm of demons is subject to Him! How then could these guys argue about greatness, when they should have been focused on Him? Can you imagine this conversation? "Jesus chose us to go up the mountain with Him, so we're obviously the leaders," the three stated. "Yeah, and I'm His favorite of the three," John added. "None of you would be here if I hadn't introduced you to Him," Philip continued. "Only a former tax collector has the leadership skills to organize a ministry like this," Matthew offered. "Roman sell-out," Simon the zealot muttered under his breath. On and on the discussion went as Jesus walked ahead. They must have lost sight of their leader momentarily.

You can be sure of this, when we start comparing ourselves to one another and sizing up our status among the fellowship of believers, we have likely lost sight of Jesus. Simply, there is no place for argument about greatness in the kingdom. Jesus is the only great one and everyone else is not. Christ followers sometimes forget that our model for living is not one another but our Lord. There's another thing these early followers missed about greatness.

MISSED POINT NUMBER TWO – Jesus is a Servant.

Both times Jesus had to remind these guys that greatness came from servanthood and both times He had predicted serving through His death! Right before they had argued on the way to Capernaum:

> Jesus said, "The Son of Man is going to be betrayed into the hands of men. They will kill him, and after three days he will rise" (Mark 9:31).

Again, right before James and John asked for places of honor Jesus predicted His death:

> "We are going up to Jerusalem...and the Son of Man will be betrayed to the chief priests and teachers of the law. They will turn him over to the Gentiles, who will mock him, spit on him, flog him and kill him. Three days later he will rise" (Mark 10:33-34).

What about Jesus giving His life away sounded like an argument for greatness?

What Jesus was trying to prepare them for was that He was taking the down elevator to the top. His greatness would not be measured in the usual way...lording over His conquered subjects. No, His greatness would come by serving those who killed Him and conquering death and the grave. Jesus was showing them the kingdom way of being great. As another illustration, Jesus pointed out a child as a model for greatness in the kingdom.

This was a hard lesson because it was counter to everything these apostles had experienced culturally. To them greatness was forcefully and aggressively pursued and maintained. To them those with power, money, and titles held sway over those who did not have these things. Not much has changed in the 2,000 years since Jesus taught about greatness. The powerful are still rich and titled power brokers who dictate what others should do. Jesus' idea of greatness hasn't changed either for He is both the greatest of the universe and the greatest servant of all. This means servanthood must mark the life of one who walks with Jesus. If you want to be great, stay close behind the master servant. All you have to do is walk in His footprints.

THURSDAY, WEEK FIVE

ARE YOU GOING TO WASH MY FEET?

"He came to Simon Peter, who said to him,
"'Lord, are you going to wash my feet?'" -John 13:6

We tend to respect people that are transparent. We pride ourselves on the motto "what you see is what you get." But is it? Is what you see in public really the same thing you'd see in private? What about behind closed doors? If so, why do people say "I wish I was a fly on the wall?"

> A.W. Tozer notes that humanity shares a "common desire to put our best foot forward and hide from the world our real inward poverty." (*Pursuit of God*, p. 107)

Often, behind closed doors we catch a glimpse of people's true heart condition, both good and bad. We've all experienced the disappointment of finding out a friend or family member wasn't who we thought they were.

At the same time, some of the most holy experiences we share happen behind closed doors. Every night, tucked away in kitchens across town, families come together to break bread, discuss the day and laugh. Behind closed doors small groups gather to study the word and "do life" together. Behind closed doors husbands and wives enjoy God's gift of intimacy. Jesus even talked about closed doors in Matthew 6:6.

> He said "when you pray, go into your room, close the door
> and pray to your Father, who is unseen."

Behind closed doors we tend to let our guard down. Whatever happens next is just a reflection of what's present in our hearts. What about Jesus? Was there ever a time He was behind closed doors and let his guard down? When Jesus was out of the limelight, away from crowds and wasn't teaching and preaching how did He treat people? Let's take a glimpse.

John 13:1 reminds us the Passover was approaching, a time to celebrate God's deliverance. Jesus and the disciples are gathered in the upper room. Tradition dictated the host would provide a servant to remove everyone's sandals and wash their feet. What might seem like a bizarre custom to us made perfect sense in Jesus' day where the primary mode of transportation was on foot. People didn't have sweat wicking socks and designer shoes; they wore crude sandals and walked long distances on dusty roads. As you can imagine, their feet were calloused, sweaty, and dirty. The problem that evening was there wasn't a servant to do this menial task. As they reclined around the table, no doubt the thought had crossed the minds of the disciples.

What happened next was revolutionary. As the disciples argued about who would be the greatest, (Luke 22:24) Jesus was about to teach them a lesson on greatness they would never forget. Richard Foster notes:

"...whenever there's trouble over who's the greatest, there's trouble over who's the least. Most of us know we'll never be the greatest; just don't let us be the least." (*Celebration of Discipline*, p. 126)

Surely this was the mindset of the disciples reclined around the table that evening. If you're honest, can you relate?

Jesus takes off his outer cloak, ties a towel around his waist and stoops down to wash the disciples' feet. The same man that forgave sins, raised Lazarus from the dead, healed the sick, cast out demons, controlled nature, multiplied bread, fish and wine, had legions of angels at his disposal, taught with authority, and confounded the religious leaders of the day. This man stooped down to wash the dirt out between his friend's toes. The silence in the room must have been deafening. This is the only time in recorded scripture Jesus verbally tells His disciples He's providing them an "example" to follow. Behind closed doors, Jesus pours out a love so radical, it could only come from another Kingdom. Peter recognized how ridiculous the situation was. There was a gross disproportion between the menial act and the greatness of the One performing it. He shouts, "Lord, are you going to wash my feet?" Peter's implication was correct. This was a completely inappropriate role reversal. Imagine the tension in the room. The disciples, fresh off an argument over greatness, were shocked and humbled by Jesus' service.

It's the same for you and me. While our feet aren't as dirty as the disciples' were, our hearts are. But Jesus sits with us all the same. Think about the first time you sat with Jesus. No doubt, after a time, He got up, took His cloak off and began to clean you. You didn't deserve it, but He did it anyway. Then, as He stood with a twinkle in His eye, He asked you to follow in His footsteps. God is changing you to look more like Jesus. As He does, don't forget to grab your towel.

FRIDAY, WEEK FIVE

WHY HAVE YOU FORSAKEN ME?

"From noon until three in the afternoon darkness came over all the land. About three in the afternoon Jesus cried out in a loud voice, "Eli, Eli, lema sabachthani?" (which means, "My God, my God, why have you forsaken me?"). -Matthew 27:45-46

Talk about your dark moments of the soul. Jesus hung there dying from His wounds. His constant companions had all but deserted Him. The public that loved Him when they needed Him now were a curious throng watching, even participating in, the public humility of this God-man. His forearm muscles balled into cramps from the spikes that severed muscles and tendons. His breathing shallow and labored as the weight of His body collapsed against the pierced limbs, disabling His ability to take a breath. His back ripped to shreds from skillful Roman torture. His head pounding from blows by the mock-scepter, from dehydration, and from lack of sleep. The other dying men on either side jeered at Him, as though they had now risen to a superior status to this pummeled piece of meat with whom they shared their execution. And yet in His agony, the final blow had not yet been dealt. Not death... the forsaking. In the darkness, Jesus cried out in His pain to His Father.

As we talk about serving like Jesus this week, we see the great cost that can come with that. Now, let's be realistic. There's a pretty good chance that none of us reading this book will be faced with such an extreme calling on our life as this. But the spirit of the sacrifice remains. What are the limits on your service to God or those you share this blue and green marble with? Maybe you've not articulated them, but in your mind you've set boundaries on your service. Perhaps you're willing to do whatever God wants you to do except... talk to that one person about God's love... or move to another country...or tithe... or give up an evening in your week to coach. If I asked you to complete this sentence what would you say: I will serve in whatever way He calls me except _____.

Jesus didn't want to go through what he went through. Before the beginning of the end, we find him in the garden dripping with bloody sweat, praying for another way. Yet the Father did not grant His request, and our Savior obeyed. Service is costly – in Jesus' case, he was to pay the ultimate price.

In that moment on the cross – a moment of darkness and agony, he quoted a portion of Psalm 22. This psalm was on Jesus' heart as He hung, dying for His family. He had served humanity and God to the ultimate degree – there was nothing more He could do. He had such agony of heart that He cried out a psalm that captured his emotional state. He felt alone... despised... overwhelmed by His human-

ness. This psalm that He reaches out to is the raw emotion of some-

one holding out hope in God alone.

> "I am a worm and not a man, scorned by everyone,
> despised by the people. All who see me mock me; they hurl
> insults, shaking their heads. 'He trusts in the Lord,' they
> say, 'let the Lord rescue him. Let him deliver him, since he
> delights in him.' Do not be far from me, for trouble is near
> and there is no one to help." (Psalm 22:6-8,11)

Today, think through the mild inconvenience that characterizes so

much of our service. Meditate on this image of Christ crying out at

His lowest moment as He served you. Let yourself find the strength

to serve at a greater cost than you are right now.

> "I want to know Christ – yes to know the power of his res-
> urrection and participation in his sufferings, becoming like
> him in his death, and so somehow, attaining to the resurrec-
> tion from the dead. Not that I have already obtained this, or
> have already arrived at my goal, but I press on to take hold
> of that for which Christ Jesus took hold of me. Brothers
> and sisters, I do not consider myself yet to have taken hold
> of it. But one thing I do: Forgetting what is behind and
> straining toward what is ahead, I press on toward the goal
> to win the prize for which God has called me heavenward
> in Christ Jesus." Philippians 3:10-14

As we look to the day that we will join Jesus in our eternal

Sabbath, may you be found in a life of service, participating in the

sufferings of Christ. Robert Moffat, a 19th century missionary to

Africa still inspires us to keep our focus in service through this famous quote:

> "We have all eternity to celebrate our victories, but only one short hour before sunset in which to win them."
> (Chris Tiegren, *At His Feet*, p. 65)

SATURDAY, WEEK FIVE

DO YOU LOVE ME?

"When they had finished eating, Jesus said to Simon Peter, 'Simon son of John, do you truly love me more than these?' 'Yes, Lord,' he said, 'you know that I love you.' Jesus said, 'Feed my lambs.' "Again, Jesus said, 'Simon son of John, do you truly love me?' He answered, 'Yes, Lord, you know that I love you.' Jesus said, 'Take care of my sheep.' "The third time he said to him, 'Simon son of John, do you love me?' Peter was hurt because Jesus asked him the third time, 'Do you love me?' He said, 'Lord, you know all things: you know that I love you.' Jesus said, 'Feed my sheep.'" -John 21:15-17

We often think of Jesus as being a great preacher filled with wisdom in His teachings. He used parables, stories, and word pictures to help those around Him understand spiritual things. However, there has never been anyone who walked this earth that has better used questions to uncover faith and understanding. (Jesus asked over 180 questions in the gospels.) Three times Jesus asks Peter: "Do you love me?" Three times Jesus answers: "Feed / take care of my sheep."

The love Jesus is referring to is an "agape" love. This kind of love is unconditional and others centered. It is a "no matter what happens" kind of love. Furthermore, Jesus defines this love as an action not an emotion. He defines loving him as feeding or taking care of His sheep. If we love Jesus then we will act like the Good Shepherd. The above interaction between Jesus and Peter will no doubt remind Peter and the disciples of Jesus' earlier teaching about being a shepherd where Jesus said:

> "I am the good shepherd. The good shepherd lays down his life for the sheep. The hired hand is not the shepherd who owns the sheep. So when he sees the wolf coming, he abandons the sheep and runs away." John 10:11-12

Unfortunately, Peter and the disciples fulfilled this Scripture and acted like a hired hand. They denied Jesus, deserted him, and hid when Satan came to attack. However, Jesus forgave them through the cross and resurrection. Now Jesus has come to restore and remind them to be shepherds of God's flock. A good shepherd is like an owner not like a hired hand. Look at the comparisons below between a hired hand and a good shepherd. (I Peter 5:2-4, John 10:1-18, and Ezekiel 34)

Hired Hand	Good Shepherd
Serves because he has to. (I Peter 5:2-3)	Serves because he wants to
Labors only for money (I Peter 5:2-3)	Labors out of love
Has no heart for the sheep (John 10:13)	Has a heart for the sheep
Leaves when trouble comes (John 10:12-13)	Gives his life for sheep
Is unfaithful to his master (John 10:12)	Faithfully serves his master
Feeds himself (Ez. 34:3)	Feeds the sheep

Allows the sheep to scatter (Ez. 34-5-6)	Searches out the lost sheep
Ruled harshly (Ez. 34:4)	Served justly
Neglects the sheep (Ez. 34:3-4)	Cares for the sheep
" " "	Delivers the captive sheep (Ez. 34:12)
" " "	Rests the weary sheep (Ez. 34:15)
" " "	Binds up the hurt sheep (Ez: 34:16)
" " "	Strengthens the weak sheep (Ez. 34:16)
" " "	Protects the vulnerable sheep (Ez. 34:17)

How do you show Jesus you love Him? Do you act more like a hired hand or a good shepherd?

> "I've learned the hard way that you can't fool people on this one. They see and smell and sense just how deep your ownership goes. They know whether you're an owner or an hourly worker – a "hired hand," as Jesus called halfhearted people who labored in the sheep-protection business of his day. You know the type: they're committed to the vision God gave them to carry out until it gets too hard, the price gets too high, the fun factor gets overshadowed by onerous challenges, and the honeymoon gets declared over and done. . . . Are you a halfhearted, low-cost hireling? Or are you a full-on owner?" (Bill Hybels, *ax.i.om*, p. 35)

If you love Jesus with an unconditional "all in" love then you will humble yourself and serve others with all your heart, mind, and strength. It will not be a half-baked effort but a full-on dedication to serve. It is the kind of service that early church leader, Francis of Assisi, had in mind when he said the following:

"Preach the Gospel to all nations, and if necessary, use words."

Reflect on the following hymn. Make it your closing prayer today.

The Shepherd Song

Chorus:
You say that you are my sheep,
why aren't you following me?
You say that I am your shepherd,
why aren't you following me?
My sheep hear my voice,
they come running to me; running to me;
and you say I am your shepherd,
why aren't you following me?

Verse 1:
I told my sheep to visit the sick
and to take the stranger in.
When you see someone who's naked,
use your wool to cover their skin;
and you say I am your shepherd,
why aren't you following me?

Chorus

Verse 2:
I told my sheep to love one another,
even your enemies too;

but you have love for only those
who have that love for you.
And you say I am your shepherd;
why aren't you following me?

Chorus

Mississippi Children's Choir; Album:
When God's Children Get Together

WEEK SIX
TO THE GLORY OF GOD

MONDAY

"May the God of endurance and encouragement grant you to live in such harmony with one another, in accord with Christ Jesus, that together you may with one voice glorify the God and Father of our Lord Jesus Christ. Therefore welcome one another as Christ has welcomed you, for the glory of God."
(Romans 15:5-7 ESV).

There is a moment in time when the demeanor of the bridal party's "best man" turns from cool and carefree to distracted and downright desperate. I've experienced this transition from various vantage points. In my twenties I had the privilege of being a grooms-man in quite a few weddings. In my thirties I began officiating wed-dings, and now in my forties I've been able to observe weddings through my wife's role as a wedding coordinator.

Somewhere between the public pronouncement at the wedding and dinner at the reception we see the mental shift of the best man. Rather than engaging in conversation and soaking up the treasured moments, this esteemed groomsman begins to rehearse (or dare I say grasp for) the content of his obligatory speech. While I have my suspicions that the father of the bride is experiencing a similar attention drift, I can only speak experientially about the mindset of the best man.

If you've been to even a handful of weddings, you can recall the times when you were moved with emotion over the eloquent words of this caring and trusted friend. Then again, you can also remember the times when the microphone should have been unplugged to rescue the crowd from the free-flowing and ill-advised reflections of a nervous groomsman.

On May 16th, 1998 it was my turn to feel the weight of delivering the speech. On that day, during the course of a touching ceremony, my brother married his best friend. And I was honored to be the best man. I'd like to tell you that I remember the wonderful food that was painstakingly prepared for the reception. It would be great to remember the words that the father of the bride shared. However, I was busy searching for a succinct way to communicate what God had laid on my heart. I was also desperately trying to avoid a fumbling, bumbling gibberish that might detract from an otherwise flawless day.

The goal of the message was to share my deep admiration for my brother and express to my new sister-in-law the significance of sharing our last name. In a moment of clarity I was reminded of two insightful Scripture references. Proverbs 22:1 reads:

"A good name is more desirable than great riches ...".

Similarly, Ecclesiastes 7:1 says,

"A good name is better than fine perfume ..."

Truthfully, I am grateful for those who bear my last name. They've carried the name in such a way that it is a joy to be associated with the name. Our parents, grandparents, aunts, uncles, and cousins have represented the name well for generations. But now the name would become better as my brother's wife would assume it. Her character would only add to the good reputation of our name and I was eager to see how she carried it. It has been about 15 years since I publicly shared this sentiment, and time has only affirmed my assumption at that time.

There's a spiritual truth here. As Christ followers, we are adopted sons and daughters of the King of Kings. Do you see the implications of sharing and bearing the name our Father has entrusted to us? We have access to a rich inheritance afforded to us as we take on His great name. We also have a profound responsibility to carry the name well as ambassadors of the name entrusted to us. It is as if God has said:

"My name is above all names. My name is exalted. It is like a strong tower. It is to be trusted and proclaimed to all generations. It is glorious and awesome. By my name you

will have authority, identity, and purpose. It is a holy name
… and it is yours."

We should be awestruck when we think of the remarkable value
of His holy name and the riches of that which has been freely given
to us. Throughout the Old Testament we read of God's zeal for His
name. Yet, no passage is more significant than Exodus 20:7. This
third commandment declares:

> "You shall not misuse the name of the LORD your God, for
> the LORD will not hold anyone guiltless who misuses his
> name."

For years I've been captivated by this passage and curious to see
how people summarize the teaching. With a measure of caution I would
like to suggest that we often miss the primary teaching of this text.

What is meant by "You shall not misuse the name of the LORD
your God"? When I ask people to give me the primary purpose of this
teaching, the vast majority of people suggest that it has something to
do with four-letter words. In short, the paraphrase usually sounds
like, "Don't swear or use profanity." But this is only a small application of a much bigger commandment.

The NIV translates the original Hebrew phrase as:

> "You shall not misuse the name of the LORD."

Comparatively, the King James version (KJV) reads:

"Thou shalt not take the name of the LORD thy God in vain."

In a similar fashion, the English Standard Version (ESV), and Revised Standard Version (RSV) all translate the text as:

"You shall not take the name of the LORD your God in vain."

The actual Hebrew word is נָשָׂא which we pronounce as nasa'. It can be defined as: to lift, to carry, to bear, or to take on. Consider the impact of reading this passage with the understanding that we "shall not TAKE ON (or CARRY) the name of the LORD our God in vain." In essence, the commandment is much more comprehensive than the four-letter word that might spill out when we stub a toe! Taking on His name is about taking on His character and echoing His nature. In a very real way, this passage in Exodus is more about ambassador-ship than language. It is about a life that emulates the Father. One small sub-section of that life is the choice of words the ambassador speaks. To bear His name is to be mindful of the comprehensive rep-utation and character of the One we represent ... and to represent Him in a way consistent with who He is.

God is vigilant about upholding His good name. Yet, He is equal-ly concerned with entrusting it to His children. What a concept! While Isaiah 42:8 explains that God will not share His glory (name) with another, 1 Peter 5:1 promises that we will share in His glory (name). These passages do not stand in opposition to one another, but as a compliment to one another. It is fascinating to note that God the Father entrusts us with His name while He empowers and implores us to carry it well.

In his book *Desiring God,* John Piper notes:

"When Scripture speaks of doing something 'for God's name's sake,' it means virtually the same as doing it 'for His glory.' The 'name' of God is not merely His label, but a reference to His character." (p. 308)

In the New Testament, we see a frequent use of the word glory. The Greek word (doxa) which is translated "glory" is utilized 168 times in the New Testament. It is defined as honor, praise, and worship. Interestingly, it originally meant "an opinion."

If "the name of the LORD" is a dominant concept in the Old Testament, "the glory of the Lord" is a prevailing theme in the New Testament. The name of the LORD will be exalted throughout eternity and He was, is, and always will be glorious. Yet, He invites His redeemed children to confidently and frequently glorify God as we bear His name!

Admittedly, we've only scratched the surface of this amazing concept of glorifying God or bearing His name in a worthy manner.

In the rest of this week's daily devotions we will explore, in more detail, the ways in which God is glorified and how we partner with Him in exalting His name.

The remainder of this chapter addresses the following:	
Tuesday: He Glorifies His Own Name	Ezekiel 36:16-38
Wednesday: We Glorify His Name	Psalm 115:1-18
Thursday: Jesus' Prayer	John 17:1-5; 22-26
Friday: When We Fall Short of His Glory	Romans 3:23
Saturday: Our Growth is His Glory	2 Peter 3:18

Perhaps the most fitting conclusion to this chapter is a prayer uttered by the Apostle Paul in Romans 15:5-7. Here, he ties together many of the themes of this book including the notion of being like Christ, serving others, and ultimately glorifying God. Let this prayer be your prayer in the days ahead as we study the culmination of our walk ... that we might glorify God.

"May the God of endurance and encouragement grant you to live in such harmony with one another, in accord with Christ Jesus, that together you may with one voice **glorify the God and Father of our Lord Jesus Christ**. Therefore welcome one another as Christ has welcomed you, **for the glory of God**." (Romans 15:5-7 ESV; emphasis mine).

TUESDAY, WEEK SIX

HE GLORIFIES HIS OWN NAME

"Therefore say to the house of Israel, 'This is what the Sovereign LORD says: It is not for your sake, O house of Israel, that I am going to do these things, but for the sake of my holy name, which you have profaned among the nations where you have gone. I will show the holiness of my great name, which has been profaned among the nations, the name you have profaned among them. Then the nations will know that I am the LORD, declares the Sovereign LORD, when I show myself holy through you before their eyes'" -Ezekiel 36:22-23

It is not an easy thing to always understand the ways of God. Lots of us could bear testimony to that truth. Take the manner in which God decided to speak through Ezekiel the prophet preacher and covenant cop. This particular pastor was to be a "living sermon" in front of God's people. This strange man, who lived in the late seventh and early sixth century BC, was a temple priest, born after Isaiah and Jeremiah, called and served in the same time period as Daniel and Habakkuk, and one of the exiles carried off from Jerusalem to Babylon during the first deportation (See 2 Kings 24:14). I know that is a lot to absorb, but the important part is the "living sermon" piece. Hang on to that for a moment.

This odd man was a prophet to the exiles. Somewhere around 572 BC, six years before Jerusalem was destroyed and surrendered into

the hands of King Nebuchadnezzar and the Babylonians, this unusual guy began to have visions from God and was called to "live out in
front of Israel" God's sermon. On one occasion he was asked by God
to make a compact clay model of Jerusalem, surrounded by siege
ramps and battering rams. Crazy stuff! Ezekiel was to lay on his left
side for 390 days, followed by 40 more days on his right side. God
asked him to put an iron pan between himself and the tiny city.
Apparently this was to be another sign of how a barrier existed
between God and His people. But here's the strangest part. This good
and righteous preacher was asked by God to eat wheat, barley, beans,
lintels, and other grains that were cooked over human excrement,
once again symbolizing the sin that marked the people of Israel.
Ezekiel protested the use of human excrement, because it would have
made him ceremonially unclean, so God allowed him to cook with
cow manure (See Ezekiel 4-5). I don't know how you hear that part
of the Ezekiel story, but I find it absolutely weird! God's thoughts are
not my thoughts and His ways are not my ways (See Isaiah 55:8). Are
you kidding me? This is not the only way in which God invited
Ezekiel into becoming "a real life message." On one occasion, God
told the prophet that his wife, the delight of Ezekiel's eyes, was going
to be taken from him as another picture of God's "living sermon" to
Israel. The prophet was instructed not to shed any tears, groan quietly, remain appropriately dressed, and tell Israel that this would be the

exact manner in which God would take away all that they cherished and delighted in (See Ezekiel 24:15ff).

The passage quoted above from Ezekiel 36:22-23 is one more example of the peculiar way God decided to preach through this prophet. Israel had failed miserably to honor the name of the LORD. She had repeatedly broken God's Law and violated her promises. So have I and so have you. God's "living sermon" through Ezekiel was to take place in a valley of dry bones. Skeleton parts were scattered everywhere. God commanded the preacher to begin to prophesy to the dry bones, so Ezekiel did. As he preached away there was a frightening noise like a rattling sound and the bones began to come together with tendons and flesh and a vast army of dead people took on new life and stood up! God was preaching through Ezekiel that He was not done with dead and hopeless Israel. God, Himself, would glorify His own name by bringing them back to life (See Ezekiel 37). The LORD would "put their lives back together," regardless of how long their sin had separated them from Him. And God by His Spirit through Jesus continues to do that same miracle. Just as God breathed on those dead bones, He breathed on the early disciples (John 20:22 and Acts 2:41), and He breathes on us the new life that only he can provide (2 Corinthians 5:17 and Galatians 2:20). He is truly preoccupied with His own glory. Oh, praise His name!

At the close of the book of Ezekiel, the "living sermon prophet" saw the glory of the LORD once again fill the temple (See Ezekiel 40-48). In our day God longs to bring the highest honor to Himself by filling our inner life, our own temple, with Himself. This highest call to cooperate with God's Holy Spirit, to walk with Him and grow in Him, in order to be changed to look like Jesus and in turn serve others in Jesus' name is not for our glory, but His and His alone.

Maybe this picture can help you see what I'm talking about. This past year a group of us from ECC drove up to the Chicago suburbs and attended the Willow Creek leadership summit. I went somewhat reluctantly, mostly due to the fact that those kinds of large conferences typically do not refresh me. A woman by the name of Mama Maggie Gobran, a Coptic Christian from Cairo, Egypt was one of the key-note speakers. Her ministry includes working among the poorest of the poor, much in the same way that Mother Teresa did in Calcutta, India. Mama Maggie shared her story, barely speaking above a whisper, sharing with us what God was doing in that part of the world and inviting us to join her in that work. She became a "living sermon." At the close of her presentation the place erupted with a standing ovation. Mama Maggie, in response, dropped to her knees and prostrated herself before us and the LORD. We wept while God glorified Himself. He longs do the same through you and me. Get the picture?

WEDNESDAY, WEEK SIX

WE GLORIFY HIS NAME

"Not to us, O Lord, not to us but to your name be the glory, because of your love and faithfulness. Why do the nations say, 'Where is their God?' Our God is in heaven; he does whatever pleases him" -Psalm 115:1-3

The first two verses of Psalm 115 begin with a very important thought for those of us who want to grow spiritually. The writer establishes right from the start who glory is not for. Our spiritual growth is not about our glory. It's not about being able to be more spiritual. Our journey of faith does not end with accolades from leaders in the church. Growing deeper is not about other believers testifying to our great spirituality. Becoming mature in Jesus is not about feeling as though we are worthy children of God. Life is not about our greatness! The writer says it twice for good measure; "not to us...not to us."

We grow spiritually for one reason and one reason only; to bring glory to God! This is a subtle but necessary thing to point out because we often miss it. In the midst of all the work the Spirit is doing in our lives, and all the ways we are becoming like Jesus, and all the serving of others, we are sometimes tempted to believe that spiritual maturity is about us. It isn't.

The word "glory" in today's Scripture (kavode in the Hebrew language) has a root word that means "to make heavy." In other words, to give glory to someone is to attach heaviness to who they are. When someone has a talent, or power, or authority, or all of these at once, we attach weight to them by glorifying them. This can either be verbal, ("Her artwork is awesome") or respectful (pulling over when a police car comes up behind you with their flashers on) or submissive (stepping aside when the tough guy is walking straight at you). All of these are ways we bring weight or glory to another. Our growing in faith is all about giving weight to God and according to the Psalmist there are four reasons He gets all the glory!

Give glory for His great love. We glorify His name because God is the greatest lover of all time. There is no one who loves like He does.

"God so loved the world" (John 3:16).

"But because of His great love for us, God...made us alive with Christ..." (Ephesians 2:4).

"From everlasting to everlasting the Lord's love is with those who fear him..." (Psalm 103:17).

"...His love endures forever" (Psalm 106:1).

"Let them give thanks to the Lord for his unfailing love" (Psalm 107:8).

I could go on and on and on, but let me ask you a few questions. Who loves you no matter what? Who loves you enough to die for you? Who loves you when you hate them? Who loves you even though they know all the bad stuff in your life? Whose love can you always depend on? The answer to all of those questions is "God."

Give glory for His faithfulness. We also glorify God's name because (He) remains faithful. Have you noticed that people are fickle? They will boo a baseball player they love if he strikes out in the bottom of the ninth inning. Good friends will dump you when you choose to not be like them anymore. Family members will get selfish if they become rich. Spouses will break their vows. Children will disobey. Christians will judge and condemn one another. Coaches will stop talking to you when you get injured. Humans are hard to rely on because they often break promises; but not God. He doesn't change. What He says He will do, He will do. Who He is, is who He has always been and will always be. When He makes a promise He keeps it. When He speaks, it is always the truth.

Give glory for His place. We glorify God for His place. The nations asked "Where is your God?" because their gods were sitting on their mantle or a nearby hill or a manmade temple. The pagan nations around Israel had gods they could see because they had made them with their own hands. They taunted Israel by questioning their God's existence. To them, if you couldn't see a god He didn't exist. The answer according to Psalm 115 is that God is too big to see. He is in heaven. He is bigger than what our hands can make. He is bigger than what our mind can understand. He is stronger than our greatest power. He is smarter than our most brilliant idea. We can't make an image of our God, He is simply too big for that. He must dwell in heaven because earth can't contain Him.

Give glory for His pleasure. We glorify God because His love, His faithfulness, and His greatness in our lives are exactly what please Him. God is the only being in the universe who does what He wants all of the time. Can you imagine if anyone else held this power? Human history has shown us what those with worldly power do. Powerful kings conquer weaker people by killing them or enslaving them. Mighty warriors overpower the enemy with the sword. Bosses will impose their will on employees. Rich will oppress the poor. Popular will reject the company of the common. God, on the other hand, uses His power to love and nurture us because He wants to!

When someone who has complete control over you chooses to love you of His own free will; there is only one appropriate response. We mature in our walk with Him so that we can glorify His name. Our only appropriate response is to worship.

THURSDAY, WEEK SIX

JESUS' PRAYER

"I have given them the glory that you gave me, that they may be one as we are one. I in them and you in me. May they be brought to complete unity to let the world know that you have sent me and have loved them even as you have loved me." -John 17:22-23

Jesus was always on time. He navigated life with an internal clock, counting down to the cross. Throughout scripture, people tried to speed up that clock and usher in the kingdom before it was time. In John 2:4, Jesus tells his own mother "My time has not yet come." A little while later, his brothers urged him to go to Jerusalem to stir up a following. Jesus' response, "The right time for me has not yet come; for you any time is right." (John 7:6) Finally, at the end of his earthly ministry, Jesus is with his disciples in the upper room. He pauses, looks toward heaven, and prays. His first words probably should have made the hair on the back of the disciples' necks stand on end; "Father, the time has come." Finally! Finally, Jesus acknowledges it's time to usher in the kingdom! It was about to get interesting.

After that initial declaration, Jesus offers one of the most comprehensive prayers in the New Testament. His prayer, capturing all 26 verses in the chapter is broken into three parts. First, Jesus prays for Himself, His authority and the work that's been completed. Then, He prays for His rag-tag group of disciples. Even after following him for years, they had no idea what was about to happen. They desperately needed His prayer covering. Finally, Jesus prays for all the believers that would come to know Him after his resurrection.

Did you notice a direct correlation in Jesus' prayer between God's glory and our unity? God, in His infinite wisdom, leverages the unity of His followers to draw others to Himself. In John 17:22-23, Jesus prays specifically for our unity **so that** two things can happen. First, our unity points people to Jesus, His life, His teaching and ultimately His death and resurrection. Our unity points people towards a savior. Second, our unity points people toward God's incredible love for them. When the church is unified, people are drawn to God and His glory. Ray Stedman has this to say about unity:

> ... it is so "unmistakable and joyful that the wordlings will envy it. Like homeless orphans with their noses pressed up against the window, they will long to join the warmth and the fellowship of the family circle." (*Talking with My Father*, p. 181)

When the church is unified, God is glorified. When the church is divided it becomes strangely irrelevant.

It's important to remember that our unity in Christ doesn't strip away our uniqueness. It actually enhances it. Unity in Christ doesn't mean uniformity. The body of Christ is a beautiful mosaic composed of different ethnicities, social classes, experiences, passions, and gifts. This diversity finds its harmony and clarity in the purposes and glory of God.

Author and Pastor John Piper has a famous saying:

"God is most glorified in us when we are most satisfied in him". (*The Dangerous Duty of Delight*, p. 21).

I'd like to add that God is most glorified in us when we, the church, are most unified in Him. Jesus knew that unity pointed to the Father's glory. He prayed so. But does this resonate in our lives? Do we treasure unity as much as Jesus and the Father? Do we protect unity as much as Jesus and the Father? Finally, do we model unity like Jesus and the Father?

We don't have to fight for unity but we do pray to maintain it. We can't manufacture it, but we can protect it. Through it all, while the world's factions clamor for attention, publicity, and relevance the church stands unified with a clear, consistent, timeless message. Jesus is the way.

FRIDAY, WEEK SIX

WHEN WE FALL SHORT OF HIS GLORY

"...for all have sinned and fall short of his glory." -Romans 3:23

"Come on in boys and get washed up for supper," my mom would call out through the kitchen window most nights. Usually you could find us boys nice and grubby from things like a good game of wiffle ball, where we typically hit the ball over the fence requiring us to sneak into Franny and Rudy's garden to retrieve our ball. But we were NOT coming to mom's supper table all covered in dirt! We were expected to show up – washed up.

It's sad, really, how many people think that's how you come to Christ too. First get your life cleaned up and then God might like you enough to embrace you like all the other "good Christian people." Show up washed up.

Well, that obviously wasn't Jesus' theology when he portrayed God in a parable as a father who kissed and hugged his manure-covered son who had finally returned home stinking to high heaven from working in pigpens. The son had carefully rehearsed his eating-crow speech, but the father wouldn't even let him finish. This father didn't expect his son to show up washed up; he cleaned him up after he came home.

In Romans chapter 3 we read that no matter how hard people tried to live righteous lives, it proved to be an impossible thing to do. "There is no one righteous, not even one." (vs. 10) I love how Eugene Peterson paraphrased Romans 3:23-24 in The Message:

> "Since we've compiled this long and sorry record as sinners (both us and them) and proved that we are utterly incapable of living the glorious lives God wills for us, God did it for us. Out of sheer generosity he put us in right standing with himself. A pure gift. He got us out of the mess we're in and restored us to where he always wanted us to be. And he did it by means of Jesus Christ."

He takes our dirty-rag righteousness, and makes us clean through His work on the cross. God's glory shines through our redemption like sunbeams through storm clouds. The impending disaster of the storm is pierced by the light of the sun. The ominous ending of eternal doom – the result of a failed attempt at self-righteous living - is replaced with an eternal glory – an unearned, undeserved gift. We would have never made it on our own. So don't try to win God's attention or favor by your own righteous living.

There are those of us who don't trust grace. We're not used to getting something with no strings attached. Frankly grace and mercy freak us out a little. Not getting what we deserve and getting what we don't deserve are nigh unthinkable to some of you.

And not only does He forgive us and cleanse us from all unright-
eousness (1st John 1:9), but He gives us the strength to live this life
He has called us to. We don't even *respond* to His glory and grace
without His help:

> "His divine power has given us everything we need for life
> and godliness through our knowledge of him who called us
> by his own glory and goodness. Through these he has
> given us his very great and precious promises, so that
> through them you may participate in the divine nature and
> escape the corruption in the world caused by evil desires"
> (2nd Peter 1:3-4).

Nothing in the gospel says "clean up your life and then we'll
talk." It's too late and "your long and sorry record" of sins is insur-
mountable. You have fallen short of God's glory – it's done. You have
to be the son in the pigpens who realizes how good it would be to be
back with the Father. Don't prepare a speech about how the father
shouldn't take you back as His child, because frankly, He doesn't
want to hear it. There's no glory restored as long as you stay in the
distant land, thinking that the Father prefers you to keep your rebel-
lious self away from Him. Don't wait until you get yourself cleaned
up, just head on back home where you are loved. Return to the Father
who wants to restore you to glory – through His own doing. As long
as you stay in the distant land, in your own self banishment, the
Father's heart breaks. Let yourself out of the pigpen prison of sin and

punishment in which you've sentenced yourself. Abandon your attempts at fixing things on your own, because that clearly is not working. Though you have fallen short of God's glory, now... God's glory is revealed through your redemption... your new destiny... your new WALK.

Saturday, Week Six

Our Growth for His Glory

"But grow in the grace and knowledge of our Lord and Savior Jesus Christ. To him be glory both now and forever! Amen."
-II Peter 3:18

I am a parent. When my kids are kind and polite to others (especially when I don't have to remind them) it pleases me. When they try their hardest in an activity or sport, it brings me joy. When my kids reach their potential, it reflects well on me as a parent. When my kids choose to consider other's interests above their own, it brings me honor. I have to be careful that this does not become a source for pride, but I am proud of my kids.

We are God's children. We are created in God's image. Similar to the illustration above, when our character reflects God's character we bring honor, joy, and recognition to our heavenly Father. In other words, when we act like God we give him glory.

When We Grow We Give Glory to God.

"This is to my Father's glory that you bear much fruit showing yourself to be my disciples." John 15:8

In practical terms, fruit represents good works - thoughts, attitudes, or actions, of ours that God values because it glorifies Him. The fruit from your life is how God receives His due honor on earth.

You bear inner fruit when you allow the Holy Spirit to shape your character.

> "But the fruit of the Spirit is love, joy, peace, patience, kindness, goodness, faithfulness, gentleness, and self control." Galatians 5:22-23

You bear outer fruit when you allow these Christ-like qualities to spill out into your behaviors which are endless in nature. Whether you are performing routine responsibilities at work, household chores, parenting duties, honey-do lists, or serving at church or in the community, all of these activities can become spiritual in nature. They all showcase God's influence (or lack of influence) in your life. And when we reflect God's nature in the way we show these behaviors, we give glory to God.

This effort we make to grow is not done in our own strength but "in the strength that God supplies, that in everything God may get the glory." (I Peter 4:11) And doing something by relying on the strength which God supplies simply means doing it by faith.

> "With this in mind, we constantly pray for you, that our God may count you worthy of his calling and that by his power he may fulfill every good purpose of yours and every act prompted by your faith. We pray this so that the name of our Lord Jesus may be glorified in you, and you in him, according to the grace of our God and the Lord Jesus Christ." II Thessalonians 1:11-12

Our "works of faith" that bring glory to Jesus are all done "according to the grace of God" because they happen "by his power." And this brings glory to the name of Jesus.

When We Focus on God's Glory We Grow.

> "And we, who with unveiled faces all reflect the Lord's glory, are being transformed into his likeness with ever-increasing glory which comes from the Lord." II Corinthians 3:18

> "The more I focus on the glory of God, the more I am changed into his likeness. We tend to become like what we admire and enjoy and the stronger the admiration the greater the influence. If the excellence of God could be admired in his pleasures, and if we tend to conform to what we admire, then focusing on the pleasures of God could help me be conformed to God." (John Piper, *The Pleasures of God*, p. 17)

There is no greater thought than what we think about God. What we think about God defines us. So there is no greater thing for us to spend time thinking about or meditating on than the character of God. And when we do this we grow to become like God and this brings him glory.

Practice focusing on the glory of God by making the following church hymn by Walter Smith your closing prayer. It is based off of I Timothy 1:17 which reads:

> "Now to the King eternal, immortal, invisible, the only God, be honor and glory for ever and ever. Amen."

Immortal, invisible, God only wise,

    In light inaccessible hid from our eyes,

Most blessed, most glorious, the Ancient of Days,

    Almighty, victorious – Thy great name we praise.

Unresting, unhasting, and silent as light,

    Nor wanting, or wasting, Thou rulest in might;

Thy justice, like mountains, high soaring above

    Thy clouds, which are fountains of goodness and love.

To all, life Thou givest – to both great and small,

    In all life Thou livest – the true life of all;

We blossom and flourish as leaves on the tree,

    And wither and perish – but naught changeth Thee.

Great Father of glory, pure Father of light,

    Thine angels adore Thee, all veiling their sight;

All praise we would render – O help us to see

    'Tis only the splendor of light hideth Thee!

APPENDIX

PRACTICING SOME OF THE CHRISTIAN DISCIPLINES

Definition: The Spiritual disciplines are *holy habits* or *practices* that are both personal and corporate *acts of devotion* that encourage spiritual growth. They don't save us, change us, or make us more spiritual than someone else. Only God does all that through Christ. The disciplines are simply *tools* that God the Spirit uses to transform us into looking more and more like Jesus. The disciplines "put us in the path" of God's grace. They can, by His grace, help increase our intention to become more and more apprentices of Jesus. Here are some examples of these disciplines, with a brief definition for each one, some Biblical passages that might help, and a few practical principles and possible resources for implementation. The reading resources are included with the most difficult listed first and the least difficult listed last. Remember that none of these disciplines are "required." These are *time-tested exercises* that many seekers of God have found to be very beneficial for their spiritual growth. Your unique personality will play a part in what disciplines you are drawn toward. Please don't forget that *every one of these habits is intended to be practiced in such a way that they prompt us and move us to serve and love others.*

<u>**Bible Intake:**</u> This is the discipline of a deliberate and prolonged intake of Scripture through hearing it, reading it, studying it, memorizing it, and meditating on it. We will talk about memorizing and meditating, as distinct disciplines, in this short list of holy habits.

Scriptures: Deuteronomy 6:6-9; 2 Chronicles 34:14-33; Ezra 7:10; Acts 17:11; and 2 Timothy 2:15, 3:16-17; and Revelation 1:3.

Principles: 1. Find the time and if you can't do that, make the time, to systematically take in the Bible. This journal can help with that step. 2. Don't be worried or preoccupied with your pace or how you compare with others. Remember that we are after transformation, not information. 3. Use a variety of means to get the Word into your interior world (note the ways already described above), even "listening" to the Word read through CD or on-line can be a powerful avenue of Bible intake. 4. When you read Scripture it is always wise to have pen and paper nearby. God often impresses something on us that we will not want to forget. 5. Find a translation that speaks your heart language. We are blessed to live in a time where there are a variety of English translations. 6. Pick a spot that allows you to give focused concentration to what you are reading. 7. Ask God to direct you toward specific applications about what you are taking in. (also see Lectio Divina)

Resources: Eugene Peterson, *Eat This Book;* Gordon Fee and Douglas Stuart, *How to Read the Bible for all it's Worth;* and Wayne Cordeiro, *The Divine Mentor.*

Celebrating and Worshiping: These disciplines invite us to praise God for who He is and what He has done.

Scriptures: Exodus 20:3; any of the thanksgiving/praise Psalms; Psalm 95:6; Matthew 4:10; John 4:23-24; Romans 12:1; Colossians 3:16; Hebrews 13:15; Revelation 4:11 and 5:12.

Principles: 1. Focus on the many attributes of God. (His goodness, kindness, righteousness, power, etc.) 2. Keep Jesus at the center of all your celebrating and worshiping. 3. Use your body as an instrument of worship and praise (one of these or a combination of lifting hands, bowing the head, falling on the knees, standing, prostrating, sitting, clapping, shouting, singing, etc.). 4. Sing to Him. 5. Use some contemporary worship CD's or DVD's to help prompt your worship. 6. Keep a good balance between public and private worship. We absolutely need both.

Resources: Paul Basden, editor for *Exploring the Worship Spectrum: 6 Views*; A.W. Tozer, *The Knowledge of the Holy;* and Joseph S. Carroll, *How to Worship Jesus Christ.*

__Confessing:__ This discipline seeks to acknowledge and admit our brokenness and sinfulness. There is another kind of confession that is addressed in the "Working and Witnessing" practice. We can confess what we believe. (Romans 10:9; Philippians 2:11; and Hebrews 3:1)

Scriptures: Leviticus 5:5, 16:20-22; Psalm 32:5; Daniel 9:4, 20; James 5:16; and 1 John 1:8-9.

Principles: 1. Try Gary Moon's 30-Day Experience, especially the part on "confession," pg. 41 in his *Apprenticeship with Jesus.* 2. Find a friend and be a friend who can receive and give confession with secrecy, grace, wisdom, and forgiveness. The often unpracticed discipline of "secrecy" comes into play. Secrecy is not only to be applied to ourselves (Matthew 6:3-4, 6:6, and 6:17-18), but to others who seek to be right with God.

Resources: See Richard Foster's wise advice on "giving and receiving" confessions in *Celebration of Discipline.* Also see John Ortberg's very practical counsel in *The Life You've Always Wanted,* chapter 7 – "Life Beyond Regret: The Practice of Confession;" and Gary Moon, *Apprenticeship with Jesus.*

Fasting: In this discipline we voluntarily deny ourselves food for spiritual purposes. Fasting is intended to be used to deny ourselves from eating, but it also could be used to deny ourselves from anything that would seek to control us. (TV, cell phones, computers, certain foods, talking, etc.)

Scriptures: Some passages to consider would include Deuteronomy 9:9; Ezra 10:6; Esther 4:16; Daniel 1:12; Matthew 6:16-18 and Acts 13:2.

Principles: 1. If you've never fasted and have a history of medical challenges, talk with a health professional first and then if they see no reason why you cannot fast, start small – a meal or two. 2. If you intend to fast more than 48 hours prepare yourself with prayer and the reduction of your food intake. 3. Pray, read Scripture, and worship during normal meal times. 4. Avoid caffeine products and juices containing acids if you are fasting more than 72 hours. 5. If you are intending to go on an extended fast, remember how you start the fast and how you come off the fast will greatly affect your experience. Light foods such as fruits or vegetable juice are wise. 6. Prepare yourself for any fast by looking at several helpful resources.

Resources: John Piper, *A Hunger for God*; Richard Foster's chapter "Fasting" in *Celebration of Discipline;* and Elmer Towns, *The Beginner's Guide to Fasting.*

Food and Fellowship: What we are talking about here is meal sharing or what some have called "fellowship meals." Before you reject this as a legitimate discipline, I would simply remind you that there is a place for fasting in the Christian life and a place for feasting in the Christian life. Jesus practiced both. The discipline is not so much in the eating part of the practice, but in the people with whom you associate and the holy conversation that follows. Sharing a meal with someone in Jesus' day was tantamount to accepting them into your life.

Scriptures: Genesis 18:1-8; Exodus 24:9-11; Isaiah 25:6-9; Matthew 11:19; and numerous passages in Luke's Gospel – 5:29-30, 7:36, 10:38-42; 11:37, etc.; and John 21:1-19.

Principles: The practice is obvious. Invite someone who is either on the "outside looking in" or doesn't have the means to reciprocate your hospitality to join you for a meal in Jesus' name and see what happens. John Wesley often reminded people that there was no personal holiness where there was no social holiness.

Resources: Leslie Hardin, *The Spirituality of Jesus* – chapter 8 – "Fellowship Meals;" though not directly about meal eating; Tan and Gregg's chapter on "Fellowship" in *Disciplines of the Holy Spirit* is very helpful in recognizing and applying the larger discipline of Christian fellowship; and see Trevor Hudson's chapter – "Belonging to the Family of God" – in his very helpful book *Christ-Following: Ten Signposts of Spirituality.*

Journaling: This discipline is closely related to prayer, study, and Christian meditation. It is the discipline of truthfully and transparently recording what God has taught us from personal reflection on daily life, Bible study, books we've read, etc.

Scriptures: Any of the Psalms could function as guides with this discipline, along with Romans 7:15-25; and 1Timothy 1:12-17.

Principles: 1. If you decide to practice this discipline, keep it simple and don't write for "publication." This is between you and your heavenly Father. 2. Avoid reading a lot of "how-to" books. 3. Find a rhythm that fits you. It is not necessary to write something every day, though there is value in that practice. 4. Seek to focus your writing on how God/His grace shows up in the daily circumstances of your life, on your Bible reflection, on things you want to remember, etc. 5. The most important principle, other than honesty, is to periodically "harvest" or go back over the things you've written down. Sometimes God speaks to us and we simply miss His articulate voice by not recalling the things that have captured our attention.

Resources: John Woolman, *The Journal of John Woolman and the Plea for the Poor*; several works by Henri Nouwen might prove helpful: *The Genesse Diary* and the *Sabbatical Journey*; and Ronald Klug, *How to Keep a Spiritual Journal.*

Lectio Divina: One of the most ancient practices of early Christians was something called "Lectio Divina." This holy habit seeks to read Scripture with a hungry and prayer-focused heart.

It has been referred to as the practice of "Sacred Reading." There are four (4) primary parts to the exercise, though some practices include five or six (Silencio-Silence at the start of the exercise and Incarnatio-Incarnation, or living out the chosen passage, at the close).

Scriptures: Same as those for "Bible Intake."

Principles: 1. Lectio (reading) – select a small Bible passage and read through it several times aloud. One verse will do. Make sure you grasp the immediate literary context. 2. *Meditatio* (meditation) – take some time to reflect slowly and carefully on the words, ideas, phrases that occur in your chosen passage. Ask questions of the text. 3. *Oratio* (Prayer) – pray what you have heard and discovered in your passage. Personalize it. 4. *Contemplatio* (Contemplation) – Many Jesus-followers have found this part of Lectio the most difficult to practice. It calls us to do nothing but sit and listen. The disciplines of silence and solitude come into play here. The idea is practice the presence of God. Give God space to speak to your heart about what you have read, meditated upon, and prayed about.

Resources: Jean Leclercq, *The Love of Learning and the Desire for God;* See Ken Boa's very fine examination of this discipline in *Conformed to His Image*, pgs. 174-186; and once again I would recommend Tony Jones, *Read, Think, Pray, Live.*

Meditating: This discipline seeks to renew the mind. It is the holy practice of filling the mind with Scripture and/or thoughts of God, His character, and His creation , while "chewing" on these things in order to gain as much from them as possible. This is not the Eastern practice of "emptying the mind."

Scriptures: Joshua 1:8; Psalms 1:2-3; Psalm 19:14; a number of verses in Psalm 119; Luke 2:51; Romans 12:1-2; and Philippians 4:8.

Principles: 1. Select a passage of Scripture to meditate upon. 2. Find practical ways, like the use of a cell phone or wrist watch, to "remind" you of what you intend to think on through the day. 3. Allow the chosen truth to sink deeply into your life. 4. Begin the day and end the day with that verse or section of Scripture in mind. 5. Use some playful and creative ways to think on the passage, such as – if it were possible to discover, what would this truth sound like, taste like, feel like, look like, etc.?

Resources: Walt Russell, *Playing With Fire: How the Bible Ignites Change in your Soul;* See Donald Whitney's superb two chapter section on "Bible Intake" – Chapters Two and Three in *Spiritual Disciplines for the Christian Life*; and Tony Jones, *Read, Think, Pray, Live.*

Praying: This is simply creating a holy conversation with God. It includes both talking and listening. Planned and structured times for this discipline can be helpful, but should not be limited to those times. We are especially after living out 1 Thessalonians 5:17 – "Pray continually."

Scriptures: There are 650 specific prayers in the Bible and at least 50 of those are significant in content and size. It is hard to narrow down a list of Scriptures but perhaps these can help: Genesis 4:26; Deuteronomy 9:25-29; 1 Kings 3:4-15; 2 Chronicles 30:18-20; Any Psalm, Daniel 9:4-19; Matthew 6:9-13; John 17:1-26; Acts 1:24-25; Ephesians 1:15-21 and 3:14-21.

Principles: 1. Speak your own heart language. Talk with God as you would your very closest friend. Remember that this is a discipline marked by a loving relationship. 2. Pray what Scripture prays. 3. Learn to listen. Too much of our praying is our talking. There must be room for quiet and intentional listening. God primarily speaks through His Word, but can speak in other ways as well. 4. If you find yourself easily distracted, write out your prayers in a journal. 5. Work at bringing balance to your life of prayer by remembering to adore

God in your prayers, by confessing your sins, and by including prayers of thanksgiving. 6. Ask according to His will.

Resources: Richard Foster, *Prayer: Finding the Heart's True Home.* Philip Yancey, *Prayer: Does It Make Any Difference?*; and Walter Wangerin, *Whole Prayer.*

Sacrificing and Serving: It is assumed that every Christian is a servant and all of us have been gifted to serve others. (Romans 12:1ff; 1 Corinthians 12:1ff; Ephesians 4:11-13; and 1Peter 4:10-11) These two disciplines are intended to be an expression of our love of God and of love for our neighbor. (Luke 10:27) Radical sacrifice is often involved in loving service.

Scriptures: Psalm 2:11; Mark 10:44-45; Luke 7:37-38, 10:30-37; John 13:14-15; Acts 9:39; Philippians 2:3-4, 2:5-11, and 2:17.

Principles: 1. Pray this simple prayer: "Father, show me who I can serve today." Watch how He answers that prayer. 2. Start with those closest to you. 3. Look for simple ways of serving others in your work place. 4. Really listen to those around you. 5. Serve someone through an anonymous act of compassion and grace.

Resources: William Watkins, "Service and Sacrifice" in *The Transforming Habits of a Growing Christian*; Chuck Swindoll, *Improving Your Serve;* and Rick Warren, *The Purpose Driven Life.*

Simplicity and Stewardship: Both of these disciplines are intended to keep us from self-gratification or raw selfishness. Simplicity calls us to willingly abstain from "gathering" more than we need. It frees us from the bondage of "things." Stewardship calls us to faithfully manage our time, spiritual gifts, and money for His glory and the benefit of others. Both habits call us to align our lives with God's purposes.

Scriptures: Deuteronomy 6:5; Joshua 24:15; Proverbs 30:7-9; Matthew 22:37-38; 1Corinthians 4:1-2, 13:1-13; 2Corinthians 8:1-5, 9:6-8; and Philippians 4:14-19.

Principles: 1. Buy things for their usefulness rather than their status. (R. Foster) 2. Avoid addictions of any kind. These are idols for destruction. 3. Create the holy habit of enjoying things without owning them. 4. Give things away periodically – clothes from your closet, books from your shelves, food from your pantry, money from your check book, etc. 5. If you are new at these two disciplines start with getting out of debt and growing toward giving 10% of your income back to the Lord. It's just a place to start.

Resources: William Law, *A Serious Call to a Devout and Holy Life;* Richard Foster, *Freedom of Simplicity;* and Mrs. Howard Taylor, *Borden of Yale.*

Silence and Solitude: These two holy habits are "companion disciplines; silence gives depth to solitude, and solitude creates a place for silence. Similarly, both of these disciplines can be practiced inwardly (whether we are with people or not) as well as outwardly." (Ken Boa, *Conformed to His Image,* pg. 88) These twin towers invite us to intentionally refrain from speaking in order to read, rest, study, memorize, meditate, pray, listen, etc.

Scriptures: Simply consider the life of Jesus – 1 Kings 19:11-13; Psalm 46:10, 62:1-2 & 5-6; Isaiah 30:15; Lamentations 3:25-26; Habakkuk 2:20; Zephaniah 1:7; Matthew 4:1, 14:23; Mark 1:35, 6:31; Luke 4:42 and 6:12.

Principles: 1. If your personality is drawn toward people rather than withdrawal from people try practicing these two disciplines in "little spaces" – five minutes here, ten minutes there. 2. Get some time away for an hour, half a day, or an entire week-end for rest and reflection. 3. Take morning or evening walks with a vow of silence in order to allow God to impress upon your heart what He desires. Don't look for something supernatural. God is always present. 4. Seek to be silent in a crowd. 5. Try not speaking for a day, unless spoken to. 6. Take a personal retreat. Runcorn and Griffin (resources below) can help you with that practice.

Resources: Henri Nouwen, *The Way of the Heart;* David Runcorn, *A Center of Quiet;* and Emilie Griffin, *Wilderness Time.*

Yielding and Submitting: These mutual practices are voluntary acts of submission in order to express our submission to Jesus and seek the highest good for other people.

Scriptures: Genesis 16:9; Matthew 5:38-42 & 43-47; Mark 8:34; Romans 13:1-5; Ephesians 5:21-6:9; Hebrews 5:7, 12:9, 13:17; James 4:7; 1 Peter 2:18, and 5:5-6;

Principles: 1. Intentionally "go second" at the grocery store, stop light, etc. 2. Look for ways of yielding to someone younger than you, not as smart as you, etc. 3. Look for things in you that you condemn in others. 4. For one day seek not to "correct" a friend, a spouse, a colleague at work, etc. who has said or done something that you felt was "incorrect." 5. Surrender "getting the last word" at work or home. 6. Pray for the well-being of political figures locally and internationally.

Resources: Leslie Hardin's chapter 5 – "Submission" – in *The Spirituality of Jesus;* the small section in Richard Foster's *Celebration of Discipline* – Chapter 8 – "The Acts of Submission;" and Leslie Hardin's chapter – "Mutual Submission: Reversing the Curse" in his marvelous work *Marriage Spirituality.*

Witnessing and Working: These holy habits are intended to guide us in investing ourselves in the life of those who do not know what God has done in and through Christ. The key here is "how" we bear witness to Jesus through what we do and what we say. The primary means is by honoring God with excellence in our work and through sharing authentic love for others.

Scriptures: Matthew 28:18-20; Mark 16:15; John 20:21; Acts 1:8, 17:22-31; Romans 1:16; Colossians 3:23, 4:5-6; and 1 Peter 3:15-16.

Principles: 1. Know God's salvation-love story and pray for opportunities to share it. 2. Look for God's answers to your prayers. 3. Ask God to give you the wisdom to know how to respond to those who don't know Him. 4. Sharpen your testimony. Think of how Paul uses his story to share Christ. (Acts 9, 22, and 26) 5. Ask your neighbors, your co-workers, your friends, etc. how you can pray for them. 6. Believe that God can use one "broken" person to save another "broken" person. 7. Let everything you do be marked by excellence and love.

Resources: N.T. Wright, *Simply Christian*; Doug Pollock, *God Space: Where Spiritual Conversations Happen Naturally;* and Bill Hybels, *Just Walk Across the Room.*

Baptism and Communion: Most of us seldom think of baptism
(immersion) and communion (sometimes called the Lord's Supper or
Eucharist) as disciplines, but they rightly belong in this discussion.
They are visible presentations of the Gospel. Baptism is a one-time
discipline, while communion is an on-going discipline. On one hand,
baptism typically marks the beginning of our faith walk. We place
our trust in the finished work of Jesus as we are buried with Him in
baptism (Romans 6:3-4). Communion, on the other hand, repeatedly
reminds us that we continually walk in deep fellowship with Jesus.
This physical meal that we regularly take together is a spiritual
reminder and celebration of Jesus' atoning death on the cross.

Scriptures: Matthew 3:1-17; 26:17-30; Mark 1:4-13; 14:12-26;
Luke 22:7-38; John 1:19-34; 13:1-38; Acts 2:38-41; 2:42-47; 8:26-
40; 9:1-19; 10:47-48; 16:11-15 & 29-34; 1 Corinthians 1:13-17;
11:17-34; Galatians 3:26-27; Colossians 2:11-12; and 1 Peter 3:21.

Principles: 1. Remember how highly the early Christians viewed
both baptism and the Lord's Supper. 2. Continually come back to the
cross and what Jesus alone accomplished in His death, burial, and
resurrection. 3. Celebrate both baptism and communion as ordinances or sacraments to be observed by the church. 4. Both disciplines give us opportunity to confess Jesus as our Savior and Lord.
5. Expect a "spiritual blessing" from the Lord as we participate in

both of these disciplines. The Holy Spirit uses these "means of grace" to convey God's blessings.

Resources: Mark Driscoll, *Doctrine: What Christians Should Believe*; Gabe Lyons and Norton Herbst, *Staying Grounded* (especially Phyllis Tickle's teaching on "Recovering the Ancient Practices"); and Donald Whitney, *Spiritual Disciplines within the Church*.

The above list of spiritual disciplines only represents a fraction of the holy habits that can be cultivated for spiritual growth in Christ. The challenge here is to grow in godly maturity. Discipline and grace are the keys. No one simply drifts into Christian growth. The two great invitations from Jesus in our journey as His apprentices are: 1. To love God and obey Him. 2. To love one another. Let these be our targets in everything we do and say (See James Wilhoit's *Spiritual Formation as if the Church Mattered*).

ANNOTATED BIBLIOGRAPHY

GOD THE HOLY SPIRIT
TAKES THE INITIATIVE

Chan, Francis. *Forgotten God: Reversing Our Tragic Neglect of the Holy Spirit*. David C. Cook, 2009.

Chan, bestselling author and much in demand preacher, wants the reader to know that the true source of the church's power is the Holy Spirit. The result of the North American church living without genuinely knowing and authentically relying on the Spirit has been catastrophic. Through a very transparent writing style, he wants the reader to know of his own desire to live in a way that can only be explained by the indwelling presence of the Spirit. Chan writes simply, clearly, and convincingly. This is a good place to start for those who have not read widely or deeply about the Holy Spirit.

Grudem, Wayne. *Systematic Theology*. Zondervan, 2000.

This is a massive resource for those who hunger to explore biblical doctrine and themes more deeply. Part 4 of this volume deals with "The Doctrines of Christ and the Holy Spirit." Well over one hundred pages are devoted to the subject, with the last section (chapter 30), exclusively given to explaining the work of the Holy Spirit. Chapter 39 – "Baptism in and Filling With the Holy Spirit" seeks to answer one of the most controversial questions many Christians struggle with – "Should we seek a baptism in the Holy Spirit after conversion?" Grudem writes humbly, competently, and powerfully. That's a rare combination.

Stott, John. *Baptism and Fullness: The Work of the Holy Spirit* *Today*. IVP, 2006 reprint.

"The Christian Life is life in the Spirit," according to John Stott. Uncle John, as he was affectionately called, died this past year, but not after completing a very long and faithful journey as a much loved and distinguished expositor, pastor, missionary, churchman, disciple, and author. His focus in this book is to help the reader have a clear biblical grasp of who the Holy Spirit is and how He is at work today.

Swindoll, Charles R. *Embraced by the Spirit*. Zondervan, 2010.

Chuck Swindoll is a well known and a much respected pastor/teacher. He has authored dozens of books and this one on the Holy Spirit has been written over decades of faithful service and personally walking in the power of the Spirit. His purpose is to invite the reader into a more intimate walk with God by having a greater understanding of the power of the Holy Spirit. This is simply an encouraging and inspiring read.

THROUGH VARIOUS MEANS

1. Relationships:

Benner, David. *Sacred Companions: The Gift of Spiritual Friendship and Direction*. IVP, 2004.

This is just a marvelous read. There are lots of books written about how God uses friendship to shape and mold us as Jesus-followers. A reader can explore classics like Francis De Sales' *Introduction to the Devout Life* and concise and contemporary works like the one by Anderson and Reese entitled *Spiritual Mentoring*. But Benner's book is currently the best of the lot. He not only tells us how friendships can be used by God to grow us, but he eloquently reveals why relationships are so vital to our journey. Benner's book could be followed up by the hungry reader with James Bryan Smith's *The Good and Beautiful Community*.

2. **Pain:**

Yancey, Phillip. *Where is God When it Hurts?* Zondervan, 2002 (25th Anniversary Edition).

Very few authors write with the sensitivity and surgical accuracy that Yancey does. This book is destined to become a classic. It originally received the Gold Medallion Award for the Best Inspirational Book of 1977. His ability to probe and question the problem of pain makes this a must read. Many others have masterfully explored the way God desires to use pain and life circumstances to change us to look like Jesus, including John Donne, C.S. Lewis, A.W. Tozer, Joni Eareckson-Tada, and William Young, but none have written as simply for our time as Yancey.

3. **Service:**

Swindoll, Charles R. *Improving Your Serve.* Word, 1981.

It is extremely challenging to pick a single resource for any subject, let alone the ocean of books that have been written on the way in which God uses service to change us into mature apprentices of Jesus. Chuck Swindoll's *Improving Your Serve*, though a little dated for the contemporary reader, still proves that it can stand the test of time. Chuck's ability to describe what the art of unselfish living looks like and how God uses it to form us into Christ-likeness is still exceptionally helpful. If the reader would like to be challenged on a larger scale toward living a very missional life then read Reggie McNeal's *Missional Renaissance*, Jossey-Bass, 2009 and others like it.

4. **Nature:**

Ford, Leighton. *The Attentive Life.* IVP, 2008.

God uses His creation to continually refine us into the people He wants us to be. Beauty, mystery, and detail all play a part in this spiritual metamorphosis. Contemporary writers like Annie Dillard, *Pilgrim at Tinker's Creek* and Fred Buechner, *Listening to Your Life*, can be very helpful in learning the way of looking and listening for evidences of God's presence. Even the non-believing David Thoreau and his *Walden* can be helpful to us. But Leighton Ford, brother-in-law to Billy Graham, born to an unmarried teenage mother, eventually adopted by a paranoid woman and a seldom present man, grew to become an apprentice to Jesus and "an artist of the soul and a friend on the journey." Leighton can help the reader become a better observer of God's presence and voice in nature.

5. Scripture:

Russell, Walt. *Playing with Fire: How the Bible Ignites Change in Your Soul*. NavPress, 2000.

"The main thing God uses to form us into the likeness of Jesus Christ is His Word..." Once again, so many other authors and books could have been included, but Walt writes with such honesty. He acknowledges that Bible reading for many of us is unexciting and hard. Repeatedly, though, he insists and seeks to show how the fiery nature of the Bible can lead to life transformation. Read Richard Foster's *Life With God*; Eugene Peterson's *Eat This Book*; Wayne Cordeiro's *Divine Mentor*, and others, but don't overlook *Playing With Fire*.

In Cooperation with Our Response
(The Practice of the Christian Disciplines)

✓Foster, Richard, *Celebration of Discipline*. Harper and Row, 1998 (20th Anniversary Edition).

This one resource has single-handedly directed and led the holy discussion of how the Spirit uses the Christian Disciplines to change us into Jesus-likeness. Many others have written extensively about the subject, but most of those contributors end up footnoting Richard's work. In this book Foster discusses and dissects twelve of the holy habits that lead us on the path to spiritual growth.

Hudson, Trevor. *Christ Following: Ten Signposts to Spirituality*. Fleming H. Revell, 1996.

If you are a global Christian, that is you like seeing how God is speaking to us through other voices outside of North America to invite us into a life of practicing the holy habits, then this South African Christian writer will be invaluable to your growth.

Ortberg, John. *The Life You've Always Wanted.* Zondervan, 1997.
John has defined this book as "Spiritual Disciplines for Ordinary People." Ortberg is simply an eloquent writer, but what he does so well in this book is place the conversation about holy habits in a context of joy and journey. He really believes that life transformation is possible and beautifully describes how these disciplines can be lived out in the "ordinariness" of our daily life.

Stevens, Paul. *Marriage Spirituality.* IVP, 1989.
If you are married and wanting to see how the disciplines can be practiced as a couple, Stevens' splendid book is a must read.

Whitney, Donald. *Spiritual Disciplines for the Christian Life.* NavPress, 1991.
If you are a practical person and want to know how the disciplines help you grow in godliness and how you begin to practice them, then this resource is for you.

CHANGES US TO LOOK LIKE JESUS

Ortberg, John. *The Me I Want to Be.* Zondervan, 2010.
Once again, John Ortberg writes about how God helps us grow and change. Perhaps a direct quote from the book will invite you to want to read it. John writes, "Here is the good news: When you flourish, you become more you. You become more that person God had in mind when He thought you up. You don't just become holier. You become you-ier. You will change; God wants you to become a 'new creation.' But 'new' doesn't mean completely different; instead, it's like an old piece of furniture that gets restored to its intended beauty" (pg. 16).

Smith, James Bryan. *The Good and Beautiful Life: Putting on the Character of Christ.* IVP, 2009.
This splendid book is the second installment in a trilogy that Smith wrote on what the Jesus-following life is really like. The other two books are *The Good and Beautiful God* and *The Good and Beautiful Community. Good and Beautiful Life* is based upon his

exploration and reflection of Jesus' Sermon on the Mount in Matthew 5-7. Dallas Willard called this volume "the best practice I have seen in Christian spiritual formation."

Stott, John R.W. *The Radical Disciple*. IVP, 2010.
This represents the last book John Stott ever wrote. His desire was to pull together a sort of "farewell speech" to the church he loved. In this final piece he explores eight of the marks of real discipleship that he thought had become neglected in the early part of the twenty-first century. This book is destined to become a classic. It is concise, clear, and especially convicting in its invitation to look like Jesus.

In Order to Serve Others

Blanchard, Ken and Phil Hodges. *The Servant Leader*. Thomas Nelson, 2003.
This co-authored book is beautifully designed, but even more than that it gets to the core question that all of us must ask: Am I a servant leader or a self-serving leader? Those who live and work in the world of business know Blanchard and Hodges are household names. Both have spent decades in the corporate world and understand the challenges of living as a life-long apprentice to Jesus.

McNeal, Reggie. *Missional Renaissance*. Jossey-Bass, 2009.
This book is a part of a very large conversation going on about the movement of the church toward greater involvement in culture and community. McNeal argues for "missional" as being a direction to go and not a place to arrive. Though some of you may not agree with everything McNeal advocates, he does rightly call us from an entirely internal focus to one with greater emphasis on the external, from program to people, and from church to Kingdom. He seeks to get to the core of servanthood.

Swindoll, Charles R. *Improving Your Serve*. Word Publishing, 1981.
This book is now three decades old, but remains a necessary read for those who want to learn to live in an unselfish way. In typical Chuck Swindoll fashion this book is anchored in solid Biblical reflection and strong practical application.

TO THE GLORY OF GOD.

Piper, John. *Desiring God: Meditations of a Christian Hedonist.* Multnomah, 2003 reprint.

Love him or dismiss him, John Piper remains one of the most influential Christian writers for those concerned about North American Christian faith. He has taught and preached for decades, mostly at Bethlehem Baptist Church in Minneapolis. He is the author of more than thirty books. This one in particular gets at the theme he loves to return to again and again – the glory of God. If you have an interest in preaching and teaching see also his work *The Supremacy of God in Preaching.*

Morgan, Christopher W. and Robert A. Peterson, editors. *The Glory of God.* Crossway, 2010.

Eight different theologians contribute to this needed book. The Glory of God is designed for those who want to explore more deeply what Scripture has to say about this critical subject. It is a bit heady at times, but nonetheless, a very helpful examination of a very grand topic.

Smith, James Bryan. *The Good and Beautiful God.* IVP, 2009.

It is hard to admit, but so many of us have misconceptions and false ideas about God. What Smith seeks to do is explore those myths and show us the God Jesus knew and revealed. The author journeys through some of the characteristics of God: His good-ness, trustworthiness, generosity, love, holiness, self-sacrificing nature and desire to change us to look like Jesus. This book is not directly about the glory of God, but leads to the reader wanting to glorify this good and beautiful God.

Works Cited

ESV. (2001). *Holy Bible*. Wheaton: Good News Publishers.

Foster, R. J. (1978). *Celebration of Discipline*. New York: Harper-Collins Publishers.

Foster, R. J. (1990). *Devotional Classics*. New York: HarperCollins.

Foster, R. J. (2008). *Life With God: Reading the Bible for Spiritual Formation*. New York: HarperCollins.

Lawrenze, M. (2000). *The Dynamics of Spiritual Formation*. Grand Rapids: Baker Books.

Miller, P. (n.d.). *A Praying Life*.

Moon, G. W. (2009). *Apprenticeship with Jesus*. Grand Rapids: Baker Books.

Mulholland, M. R. (1993). *Invitation to a Journey*. Downers Grove: InterVarsity Press.

Mulholland, M. R. (2000). *Shaped by the Word*. Nashville: Upper Room Books.

NIV. (1984). *Holy Bible*. International Bible Society.

Nouwen, H. (2006). *Spiritual Direction*. New York: HarperCollins Publishers.

Nouwen, H. (2004). *Out of Solitude: Three Meditations on the Christian Life*. Ave Maria Press.

Ortberg, J. (1997). *The Life You've Always Wanted*. Grand Rapids: Zondervan.

Pascal, Blaise. *Thoughts*, translated by W. F. Trotter. Vol. XLVIII, Part 1. The Harvard Classics. New York: P.F. Collier & Son, 1909–14; Bartleby.com, 2001. www.bartleby.com/48/1/.

Peterson, E. (2005). *The Message*. Colorado Springs: NavPress.

Peterson, E. (2007). *The Jesus Way*. Grand Rapids: Wm. B. Eerdmans Publishing Co.

Piper, J. (2001). *The Dangerous Duty of Delight*. Sisters: Multnomah Publishers.

Piper, J. (2986). *Desiring God.* Colorado Springs: Multnomah.

Piper, J. (n.d.). *The Pleasures of God.*

Rather, Dan. Interview with Mother Teresa, transcript. http://philfox rose.com/tag/mother-teresa-of-calcutta/

Sanders, J. O. (1967). *Spiritual Leadership.* Chicago: Moody Bible Institute.

Spurgeon, C. H. Sermon delivered on April 11th, 1880 at the Metropolitan Tabernacle, Newington, England http://www.spurgeon. org/sermons/1532.htm

Stedman, R. C. (1997). *Talking with My Father.* Grand Rapids: Discovery House Publishers.

Swindoll, C. (n.d.). *Come Before Winter.*

Tiegreen, Chris. *At His Feet.* (2003) WALK THRU THE BIBLE.

Tozer, A. (1978). *God's Pursuit of Man.* Camp Hill: Wing Spread Publishers.

Various. (1999). *The Spiritual Formation Bible.* Grand Rapids: Zondervan.

Whitney, D. S. (1991). *Spiritual Disciplines for the Christian Life.* Colorado Springs: NavPress Publishing.

Willard, D. (1997). *The Divine Conspiracy.* New York: Harper-Collins Publishers.

Willard, D. (2006). *The Great Omission.* New York: HarperOne .

Yancey, P. (1995). *The Jesus I Never Knew.* Grand Rapids: Zondervan.

WALK
Study Guide

INTRODUCTION

Thank you for your willingness to participate in this study! Our hope and prayer is that this curriculum will be a great tool for you and your group as you walk together in this journey of spiritual formation.

As you travel together in your small group through these six sessions, we are confident that God will continue to transform you into the image of His Son as you draw nearer to Him and to one another.

In order to get the most out of this study, please review each session prior to meeting as a group.

Additionally, please familiarize yourself with the Appendix and Annotated Bibliography. Each will provide breadth and depth to your understanding and application as we journey through this study together. Be encouraged as you prepare for each weekly study. Your thoughtful participation will be a blessing as you interact with God's Word and one another!

In Christ,

Jim Probst

Pastor of Small Groups
Eastview Christian Church
www.eastviewchurch.net

WEEK ONE

GOD THE HOLY SPIRIT TAKES THE INITIATIVE

DISCUSSION STARTERS: (SELECT ONE)

1. If this is a newly-formed group, have everyone introduce themselves. Briefly share about your family, hobbies, and what you hope to gain by being a part of this group.

2. If this is a pre-existing group, share briefly about your first kiss. Who took the initiative?

KEY WORD STUDY:

Peripateo: This Greek word communicates a vivid word picture in the New Testament that is translated as "live" in the NIV and translated as "walk" the ESV. Peripateo means "to make one's way or to progress; to make due use of opportunities."

KEY SCRIPTURE:

"But the Counselor, the Holy Spirit, whom the Father will send in my name will teach you all things and will remind you of everything that I have said to you" (John 14:26)

SOUND BITES:

- "For all things God is the great Antecedent." A.W. Tozer, _God's Pursuit of Man_
- (Regarding John 14:26) "Let me set the context. It is Passover, Jerusalem, they've borrowed an upper room, Jesus and the twelve have. This is a part of Jesus' farewell speech. He's just finished washing the disciples' feet and He's predicting His own betrayal.

And these four key words that I'm going to talk about: teach, reminds, guides, and convicts all show up here. So let me read these." –J.K. Jones

- "If the Holy Spirit is not at work the world comes to an end. An abrupt end. So there's no hope. There's no way that we can possibly mature, grow, walk with Jesus (believer, not a believer) unless the Holy Spirit is active. That's why we started with that key statement, that God the Holy Spirit takes the initiative. It's not our idea." –J.K. Jones

- "I can take a deep breath and just know that the Holy Spirit is doing some deep stuff in my heart right now because I am a follower of Jesus Christ and I have faith in Him and His Spirit is illuminating and teaching and convicting and guiding ... As we are going to learn in the future weeks is all we have to do is get in concert with what He's doing." –Mike Baker

DISCUSSION:

1. Select one of the "Discussion Starters" above and share your response with one another.

2. Have someone begin this study by leading the group in prayer.

3. Introduce the "group covenant" to all of the group members and discuss some basic expectations for the group.

4. Read the "key word study" and discuss the big idea of this six-week study entitled "WALK" (see the overview in the book for more insight).

5. Review the definitions of spiritual formation in the overview at the beginning of this book. Which definitions do you find most helpful?

6. Watch the video segment for session one entitled "God the Holy Spirit Takes the Initiative."

7. Take a moment to read / review the "sound bites" in this session. What was the most insightful or impactful comment you read or heard on this subject?

8. As a group, read John 14:26, John 16:13, and Ephesians 1:17-18. What words describe the Holy Spirit's work in these passages? How have you seen these key verbs lived out in the church?

9. The Holy Spirit teaches, reminds, guides, illuminates, convicts, searches, testifies, helps, intercedes, and fills. Which of these 10 "initiatives" have you most recognized in your life? Explain.

10. Consider the daily devotions for this week. Which of these writings is most intriguing to you? Why?

11. Review the last "sound bite." Does this concept provoke ease or effort for you? Explain.

12. To summarize, **"God the Holy Spirit takes the initiative"** in our faith journey. Are you most likely to focus on His initiative in your past, present, or future? Explain.

13. What questions about His initiative remain unanswered at this time? How can the group help?

14. Pray together as a group.

BETWEEN THE MEETINGS:

1) Take time to reflect on the 10 words that describe the Holy Spirit's initiative in our lives (listed in Monday's daily devotional for week one). Examine your "walk" and His initiative as noted in these 10 key words. Journal about the activity you recognize as He initiates spiritual growth in you.

2) Continue in your daily reading of "WALK".

3) Attend next Sunday's service to learn about the "various means" by which the Holy Spirit most often takes the initiative.

4) Pray that the members of your group grow closer to Christ and one another through this study.

NOTES AND PRAYER REQUESTS

"THROUGH VARIOUS MEANS"

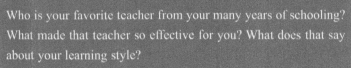

DISCUSSION STARTERS: (SELECT ONE)

Who is your favorite teacher from your many years of schooling? What made that teacher so effective for you? What does that say about your learning style?

Have each person share their most memorable vacation experience.

KEY WORD STUDY:

Hypomonē: In the first chapter of James, this word is translated as "perseverance." It is the final word of verse 3 and the first word of verse 4. It conveys the idea of endurance, steadfastness, and patience. Regardless of the "various means" God employs, we can respond with perseverance of faith and enjoy the process of maturation.

KEY SCRIPTURE:

"Consider it pure joy, my brothers, whenever you face trials of many kinds, because you know that the testing of your faith develops perseverance. Perseverance must finish its work so that you may be mature and complete, not lacking anything." (James 1:2-4)

SOUND BITES:

- "At the risk of sharing the obvious, God is a world class communicator. The connection is critical. The cost is great. He purchased access and paved the way to our hearts ... clinging to a rugged cross. God the Father is using the finished work of Christ and the ongoing work of the Holy Spirit to capture our attention. He uses various means to reach people with the loving message of salvation. He continues to communicate through various means to cultivate lives that radiate the reality of Christ ... While the cross is central to each story, you will likely hear creative combinations of the five means we will discuss in the coming segments of this book (relationships, pain, service, nature, and Scripture). These are languages that God skillfully and lovingly speaks into our lives to address us in our darkest hours, our most defiant times, and when we are longing for His presence. Our *walk* is dependent upon clear communication, and God is speaking." Jim Probst

- "What James is teaching is shocking – God uses pain as a tool to glorify Himself and mature us. Pain and spiritual growth are inseparable." J.K. Jones
- Referencing James 1:27, Mike Baker noted, "The word pure had the idea of the Old Testament priest getting ready to go in and serve at the temple. He had to be pure, cleansed, purified. This other word has, the faultless word, behind it the idea of not having a stain. It is a "dyeing" from the Old Testament, like your dyeing colors of clothes. And so, He says if you really want to express true Christianity in this world today, something this pure before God, and something that is not stained, learn how to serve other people."
- "...examine your own life and ask yourself how is it that the Holy Spirit has used pain in your life to change you. Or relationships. Or the word of God. Or any of the other things that we've talked about in your reading and in the Scripture that we've studied this week. I found in my spiritual walk the best way for me to understand what God is doing is to look backwards and see that the Holy Spirit has used those things to make me who I am and to embrace them and then to be able to move forward - understanding that He is going to continue to work in that way." Mike Baker

DISCUSSION:

1. Select one of the "Discussion Starters" above and share your response with one another.?
2. Have someone begin this session by leading the group in prayer.

3. Watch the video segment for session one entitled "Through Various Means."

4. Take a moment to read / review the "sound bites" in this session. Which comments or insights (from the book, sound bites, or video teaching) have made the greatest impression on you thus far?

5. Read James 1:2-27 as a group, noting the "various means" expressed in the passage.

6. In his daily devotional for this week, Tyler Hari writes, "It feels counter-intuitive to think God speaks clearly to us while we serve others. When serving others, our focus isn't on ourselves but other people, and we hardly expect to hear from God then. Yet, that's right where God wants us! As we serve others, God speaks to us about previous hurts, future decisions, present anxieties, and areas of growth in our lives. As we serve others, we loosen the grip on our own personal agendas with God and make room for Him ... and God speaks." How has your walk matured through service?

7. Jason Smith notes the following about the means of nature: "Nature communicates. It speaks to us through avenues not limited by words. It points us to God and reveals His eternal power and divine nature (Romans 1:18). It counsels us to put our trust in God rather than our own means ... Nature reminds us of who we are and our place within this planet as caretaker and authority (Genesis 1:28-31). It also reminds us of who we are *not*, by the vastness and wisdom of all creation." In what ways has nature been used by God to communicate to you?

8. Regarding the *means* of Scripture, Mark Warren says, "The Psalms are filled with miniature love letters to God and from God. They reveal raw emotions and life changing truths." In what specific ways have you encountered the Living God through His Word? Explain.

9. Re-read the final sound bite in this study. As you look back to the *various means* God has used to communicate with you, what do you notice about your receptivity? Which *means* speak loudest in your life?

10. The five means we have listed in this study are not an exhaustive list of ways in which God communicates with us, but they are probably the most common. Are there other *means* that God has used to take initiative in your life? Explain.

11. Pray together as a group. Ask each member of the group to write one of the *means* on a notecard and place it at their feet (refer back to #8 in the discussion). As a group, pray for each member to see God at work through those particular means.

BETWEEN THE MEETINGS:

1) Consider graphing or noting the times in your life when you experienced the greatest pain (physical, emotional, etc.). On the same graph, note the intimacy of your walk with Christ. Is there a correlation worth noting?

2) Continue in your daily reading of "Walk." Look for ways to discuss what you are learning around the dinner table at least one night this week.

3) Pray for the members of your group that they might grow through pain, relationships, nature, Scripture, and service.

4) Study James 1:2-27, noting how *God the Holy Spirit takes the initiative through various means.*

NOTES AND PRAYER REQUESTS

"IN COOPERATION WITH OUR RESPONSE"

DISCUSSION STARTERS: (SELECT ONE)

1) Describe the best teamwork you have ever experienced.

2) Write the name of your favorite TV show on a piece of paper. Collect the papers and read each one, guessing which person wrote each answer.

KEY SCRIPTURE:

"Let us draw near to God with a sincere heart in full assurance of faith, having our hearts sprinkled to cleanse us from a guilty conscience and having our bodies washed with pure water. Let us hold unswervingly to the hope we profess, for he who promised is faithful. And let us consider how we may spur one another on toward love and good deeds. Let us not give up meeting together, as some are in the habit of doing, but let us encourage one another – and all the more as we see the Day approaching." Hebrews 10:22-25 (emphasis mine)

KEY WORD STUDY:

Paroxysmos: this word is translated as spur, provoke, stimulate, or motivate in our English translations of Heb. 10:24. It can be defined as an inciting or an irritation. Simply put, when we are called to "spur one another on" – we are called to be "holy irritants" that provoke or incite others to faithfulness!

SOUND BITES:

- "We can't just sit back and say, 'Hey, Holy Spirit, do your thing.' So today we're going to ask how is it that we can cooperate? What could we do to get on board with how He's growing us? There are some things that we could do individually (that's what our reading is about this week), but also there are some things that we can do together." Mike Baker

- "...but there's another side to confession and you hear some of that in verse 24. Again, 'let us consider how we may spur one another on toward love and good deeds.' It is not just the sin, but it is our faith in Christ that we confess to each other. In some way we cheer, that word spur, in some ways without stretching it, it is like spiritual trash talking positively. We're inciting each other." J.K. Jones

- "... my mind races to the cross. I always think about it in terms of I Corinthians 11 when Paul was rehearsing what Jesus did for us. So we have these beautiful pictures of things that we do together. Our baptism reminds us of our commitment and communion reminds us of Jesus' sacrifice, His faithfulness." J.K. Jones

- "What we're really talking about is creating space in our lives for God's influence to take root. Generally speaking, these *availabilities* are known as spiritual disciplines." Jim Probst

DISCUSSION:

1. Select one of the "Discussion Starters" above and share your response with one another.

2. Have someone begin this session by leading the group in prayer.

3. In our study today we will make a subtle transition from awareness of God's initiative to our availability in cooperation with Him. Take a moment to discuss some of the things you've already read and/or practiced in your walk with Christ that make you more available to His leading.

4. As you discuss some of the "disciplines" or "availabilities" that you are familiar with, note that some are to be practiced in community while others are to be practiced individually. Our video

teaching today will emphasize communal practices while the daily devotionals emphasize individual practices. Which most naturally come to mind for you?

5. Watch the video entitled "In Cooperation with Our Response" as a group.

6. Read Hebrews 10:19-25 as a group, preferably from two different translations.

7. The video teaching and Hebrews 10:22-25 highlight the following "communal disciplines:" baptism, communion, celebration, worship, fellowship, and confession. Which of these are most impactful in your *walk*? Why?

8. Take a moment to read / review the "sound bites" and reflect on the teaching in this session. What was the most insightful or impactful comment you have read or heard in this session?

9. There were various "disciplines" discussed in this week's daily devotionals: Bible intake / Meditation, Repentance / Confession, Witness / Work, Solitude / Silence, Stewardship / Simplicity. Which one is least familiar to you? How would things change if you would make this discipline a priority?

10. Quickly review the appendix in this book. Which spiritual disciplines have you given little attention to in the past? What insights have you gained in working through this list?

11. When you think about our "cooperation" with the Holy Spirit, what descriptive term best expresses your understanding of our "response?" A) Holy habits; B) Spiritual disciplines; C) Availabilities; D) Spiritual training; E) Other

12. Pray together as a group. Consider using the content of Hebrews 10:22-25 as an outline for your closing prayer.

BETWEEN THE MEETINGS:

1) Read through Acts 2 and note all of the spiritual disciplines that were practiced in community with the early church. Is there anything lacking in our church community? Is there anything we excel in practicing?

2) Continue in your daily reading of "WALK."

3) Pray that the Lord helps you and your group members to build holy habits both individually and corporately as you "cooperate" with His work in your life.

4) Look ahead to "discussion starter" #2 for next week. Plan accordingly!

NOTES AND PRAYER REQUESTS

WEEK FOUR

"CHANGES US TO LOOK LIKE JESUS"

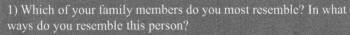

DISCUSSION STARTERS: (SELECT ONE)

1) Which of your family members do you most resemble? In what ways do you resemble this person?

2) Have each member bring a photo of themselves from their early childhood or infancy. Mix them up and try to guess which photo corresponds with each group member.

KEY SCRIPTURE:

"And we, who with unveiled faces all reflect the Lord's glory, are being transformed into his likeness with ever-increasing glory, which comes from the Lord, who is the Spirit." 2 Corinthians 3:18

KEY WORD STUDY:

Metamorpho: This word is translated as "transformed" in 2 Corinthians 3:18 and it conveys the idea of being changed into an entirely different form (metamorphosis). Matthew 17:2 and Romans 12:2 also use this word to convey dramatic change in both Christ and His followers.

SOUND BITES:

- "The *literal* truth is that Christ through His word removes the old routines in the heart and mind – the old routines of thought, feeling, action, imagination, conceptualization, belief, inference – and in their place he puts something else: *His* thoughts, *His* attitudes, *His* beliefs, *His* ways of seeing and interpreting things, *His* words." Dallas Willard, *Hearing God*

- "So the question for us today is: are we beginning to resemble Jesus? Are there things in your life that resemble what He was like? ... The question for today is do we look like Jesus spiritually?" Mike Baker
- "So there is something about chapter 3 [of Colossians] that speaks to this thing of learning to live like Jesus, look like Jesus. I'm going to carve this up into three pieces ..."
- "So in the first four verses Paul seems to be saying live like a dead person." What does this mean for us? [Colossians 3:1-4]
- "So he is saying in this second slice of Colossians 3 – 'get serious about sin'." [Colossians 3:5-11]
- "So let's label the third part 'dress for success'." [Colossians 3:12-17]
- "... sometimes we focus so hard on the old clothes we're trying to get rid of, that they become dominant in our thoughts and our hearts and our souls and we can't get past them. The best thing we can do is to put on ... the clothing of Jesus Christ ... because the more you focus on that you're going to start to dislike the old clothes. The more you wear the new suit, you're not going to put on the old stuff because you look better, you're looking more like Jesus Christ every day." Mike Baker

DISCUSSION:

1. Select one of the "Discussion Starters" above and share your response with one another.?

2. Have someone begin this session by leading the group in prayer.

3. God the Holy Spirit takes the initiative, through various means, in cooperation with our response, and changes us to look like Jesus in order to serve others to the glory of God. Today we are talking about being changed to look like Jesus. Before watching the video, please read Colossians 3:1-17 together as a group.

4. Watch the video segment entitled, "Changes Us to Look Like Jesus."

5. What stood out to you as the most significant point in this video today?

6. Take a moment to read / review the "sound bites" in this session. Do you resonate with the final sound bite in this section? Explain.

7. Is it easier for you to "put off" the old ways or to "put on" the new ways that are addressed in Colossians 3? Explain.

8. Take a moment to think about your *walk* over the past 5 years. In what areas have you seen the most growth / change?

9. In your daily reading this week we are focusing on "the Beatitudes." The five we've written about are:
    Blessed are the poor (Matthew 5:3)
    Blessed are those who mourn (Matthew 5:4)
    Blessed are the meek (Matthew 5:5)
    Blessed are those who hunger and thirst (Matthew 5:6)
    Blessed are those who are merciful (Matthew 5:7)
    In which of these areas do you look the least like Jesus today? Explain.

10. Take a moment to highlight the Scripture references from Saturday's devotional for this week. As you review them, consider the immense mercy that God has shown each of us.

11. Share examples of God's rich mercy with one another.

12. List a variety of attributes of Christ as a group. Then select the one attribute that you feel most compelled to prayerfully emulate this week.

13. Pray together as a group, asking God the Father to transform you into the image of the Son through the power of the Spirit.

BETWEEN THE MEETINGS:

1) Use a dry erase marker to write 2 Corinthians 3:18 on your bathroom mirror. Meditate on this passage daily throughout the week.

2) Continue to explore ways of incorporating spiritual disciplines into your routine.

3) Pray for one another and encourage one another when you see Christ-like characteristics revealed in your fellow group members and family members.

4) Continue to read "WALK" daily.

NOTES AND PRAYER REQUESTS

"In Order to Serve Others"

DISCUSSION STARTERS: (SELECT ONE)

1) Describe your first car on a piece of paper. Redistribute the descriptions and read them aloud, guessing whose car is being described.?

2) What is your favorite book of the Bible? Why?

KEY SCRIPTURE:

"Your attitude should be the same as that of Christ Jesus: Who, being in very nature God, did not consider equality with God something to be grasped, but made himself nothing, taking the very nature of a servant, being made in human likeness. And being found in appearance as a man, he humbled himself and became obedient to death – even death on a cross!" Philippians 2:5-8

KEY WORD STUDY:

As seen in Philippians 2:7, the word "servant" comes from the Greek word "*doulos*" which is synonymous with "slave" and "bondman." Note the use of this word in Matthew 25:23, Mark 10:44, Romans 6:19, and 1 Corinthians 12:13 for a better understanding of the expanse of this significant word.

SOUND BITES:

• "… those places you walk into sometimes that are big on hospitality and have those buttons, you know those badges that say 'I'm here to serve you.' That really should be implanted on the soul of every Christian person, 'I'm here to serve you.'" Mike Baker

- "It is coming back to this very simple thing of radical servanthood. Jesus empties Himself. Without this (here is the critical part for me), if there is not that emptying, when I am preoccupied with others around me, then there can be no filling of the Spirit. There's no room for those two things to coexist." J.K. Jones

- "The word 'obedient' means to come within listening distance of the Father's voice. Not my will but Yours be done. That's the language here. So He gives ear to God, He listens and carries out this servanthood which ultimately leads our Savior to the cross. That's the language. That's our calling in some way to take up our cross every day." J.K. Jones

- "In our next lesson we'll talk about the glory of God the Father, but now we are getting to this economy in Jesus and the Jesus following way that is totally counter to our culture. In our culture if you want to be great you go for it. If you want to be number one you pursue it. But in Jesus' economy if you want to be great you are the servant of all. If you want to be first you're last. If you want to make your name great you become nobody ..." Mike Baker

- "And so if we are going to be formed in the image of Jesus Christ and we're going to be followers of Christ, we're going to walk this journey, and the path to greatness is a downward path for servanthood." Mike Baker

DISCUSSION:

1. Select one of the "Discussion Starters" above and share your response with one another.?

2. Have someone begin this session by leading the group in prayer.

3. Watch the video segment entitled "In Order to Serve Others."

4. As you contemplate the main points of the video teaching, take a moment to read Philippians 2:3-11 as a group.

5. Notice that this section of Scripture emphasizes service to others and culminates in "the glory of God the Father." We will address

"glorifying God" next week. For now, what does this passage (and the video teaching) highlight about serving?

6. In this Saturday's daily devotional, Mark Warren notes, "If you love Jesus with an unconditional 'all in' love then you will humble yourself and serve others with all your heart, mind, and strength. It will not be a half-baked effort but a full-on dedication to serve. It is the kind of service that early church leader, Francis of Assisi, had in mind when he said the following, 'Preach the Gospel to all nations, and if necessary, use words.'" How have you seen the members of your group "preach" through service? Share some encouraging observations with one another.

7. Read the first verse of Romans, Philippians, Titus, and Philemon. What do these initial greetings reveal about Paul's perspective and identity in Christ?

8. Read the third "sound bite" from this study. In what ways are you coming within "listening distance of the Father's voice?" How does this relate to two weeks ago when we studied "In Cooperation with Our Response?" Explain.

9. If your small group has been together for a while, how have you served together? Looking forward (new or existing group), how might your group serve together in the church or beyond the church walls?

10. What additional practices or principles might be helpful for you and your group as you contemplate a faith-filled response to this teaching?

11. Pray together as a group.

BETWEEN THE MEETINGS:

1) Take inventory on the formal and informal ways in which you serve, both individually and as a family and small group.

2) Think back to our second week in this study. Is service one of the ways in which God has taken the initiative in your life? Are you more likely to sense His leading while you are serving?

3) Prayerfully seek opportunities this week to serve someone within the church and someone outside of our faith community.

4) Continue to read "WALK" and preview the upcoming study entitled "To the Glory of God."

NOTES AND PRAYER REQUESTS

"TO THE GLORY OF GOD"

KEY SCRIPTURE:

"who is a deposit guaranteeing our inheritance until the redemption of those who are God's possession - to the praise of his glory." Ephesians 1:14

KEY WORD STUDY:

Doxa: Our English equivalent to the Greek word "doxa" is "glory." Glory is one of the great images employed to capture the stories of the Bible. The NIV references glory 275 times. It conveys the idea of splendor, magnificence, beauty, and radiance. "It combines awe and terror, and it simultaneously invites approach and distance." (Dictionary of Bible Imagery, p. 330).

SOUND BITES:

- "To me that is the surprising thing about spiritual formation - that spiritual formation is not about me feeling better about myself, more righteous, more holy, a better Christian, a different grade of Christian. Everything is about the glory of God." Mike Baker

- "We ourselves say yes and I believe in Him and I want to walk with Him. There is no better letter in the New Testament speaking of this *walk* metaphor. Then the last part is that "marked" language. "You were marked in him with the seal, the promised Holy Spirit, who is the deposit guaranteeing your inheritance." So, seal is that mark of ownership. Paul is saying I belong to Him, you belong to Him. Don't walk unless you have that relationship with Him." J.K. Jones

- "Hopefully we're maturing in Christ because this God that we want to give glory to, started it all by saying 'You know what? I chose you. And I want you and I want you to live within this will, these parameters, these boundaries that I've established. And not only that but I am going to do the work of Jesus Christ and I am going to secure all that I am deciding to do in your life. I am going to make it happen through Jesus. Then I am going to give you the Holy Spirit to do all this formation stuff that we're talking about, and to guarantee what's coming. In other words, why wouldn't we glorify Him? He's done all the good stuff; He's done all the good work." Mike Baker

DISCUSSION:

1. Select one of the "Discussion Starters" above and share your response with one another.?

2. Have someone begin this session by leading the group in prayer.

3. As a group, read Ephesians 1:1-14 (noting His initiative and glory).

4. Watch the video segment for session one entitled "To the Glory of God."

5. Take a moment to read / review the "sound bites" in this session. What element of God's glory most impacted you?

6. Revisit Monday's daily devotional for this week. How does the name of God interact with the glory of God? Do His children, who bear His name, have the responsibility and privilege of glorifying His name? Explain.

7. In Friday's daily devotional from this week we read of "When We Fall Short of His Glory." Have someone in the group discuss the significance of Romans 3:23 and Romans 6:23 in light of His glory and our responsibility.

8. Read 2 Peter 3:17-18 as a group. In what ways does this brief passage capture the essence of this entire study?

9. Looking back in Ephesians (and the introduction to this entire study), make note of the seven verses that address our "walk" in Ephesians: 2:1; 2:10; 4:1; 4:17; 5:2; 5:8; 5:15. Which one speaks loudest to you in this season of your journey with Christ? Why?

10. As we summarize the entire "WALK" study, discuss the definition we have been using to guide our discussion: "God the Holy Spirit takes the initiative, through various means, in cooperation with our response and changes us to look like Jesus in order to serve others to the glory of God." When you consider the broad topic of spiritual formation, are there any significant elements missing from this definition? Are there other elements that should be addressed?

11. Throughout the six sessions of this curriculum, what has been the most significant chapter for you? Explain.

12. Pray together as a group.

BETWEEN THE MEETINGS:

1) Take time to reflect on your experience throughout this study. *God the Holy Spirit takes the initiative through various means, in cooperation with our response and changes us to look like Jesus, in order to serve others, to the glory of God.* Before closing this book and moving on to another study, plan a solitude retreat where you can further reflect on God's initiative (week one) and your response (week three). How might you build "holy habits" into your life in the coming months and years (serving others to the glory of God)?

2) Consider reaching out to a member of your small group to schedule ongoing spiritual formation "check-ups," using the six segments of this study as your discussion points.

3) Look to continue in community with this small group or a new group as you begin another study.

NOTES AND PRAYER REQUESTS

THANK YOU FOR WALKING
THROUGH THIS STUDY
WITH ONE ANOTHER!

About the Authors:

The writing team from Eastview Christian Church is comprised of six men who love and cherish their Father, their families, their ministry, and one another. Each of these men has written one of the daily devotionals for each of the six studies in this book. In addition to leading their specific areas of ministry, they also contribute to an online daily devotional at www.eastviewchurch.net.

Mike Baker	Senior Pastor
Tyler Hari	Pastor of Outreach
J.K. Jones, Jr.	Pastor of Spiritual Formation
Jim Probst	Pastor of Small Groups
Jason Smith	Pastor of Family Ministries
Mark Warren	Executive Pastor

GROUP CONTACTS:

Name   Phone   Email Address

_____

_____

_____

_____

_____

_____

_____

_____

_____

_____

_____

_____

_____

_____

_____

Conclusion

Every walk comes to a conclusion. Years ago, while stationed in Germany, I recall how much I loved seeing all the families enjoying their Sunday walk. It didn't seem to matter if the weather was good or bad, people were out and about. I was usually a bit disappointed when the day drew to a close and families returned home. Whether we are taking a stroll through the neighborhood, on a forced march, or heading down to the local coffee shop, eventually we reach the intended destination. There are exceptions, of course. An accident can occur. As unlikely as it seems, a driver now and then loses control of their car and crashes into an innocent pedestrian. Heart attacks, pulled-muscles, or even something as gentle as a neighborly conversation can keep us from finishing our walk. You get the idea. The walk described in this study is not an aimless one or a leisurely Sunday jaunt. It is, by Biblical understanding, marked by great intentionality and perseverance. Each one of the six primary themes discussed is intended to coach each of us to walk *the walk* in order to grow into Christ-likeness. The question in closing is fundamental. How do we finish the walk well? There are some specific steps that can be taken.

First, we accept the finished work of Jesus Christ. Before we can finish well, we confess that He finished well. The health and vitality of our walk depends on our trust in Him, not ourselves. He offers us the gift of His accomplished work on the cross and we simply accept it with gratitude, joy, and faith. We confess with our mouth what we have believed in our hearts that He alone is Lord (Romans 10:9). He is, after all, the author and perfecter of our faith (Hebrews 12:2). Our call is to not take our eyes off of Jesus as we journey with Him. This is why we can embrace the notion that God the Spirit is taking the initiative in our life. He is powerfully at work, because God the Son is powerfully alive in us. So, here is the first and essential question, have I surrendered to Him? If not, my walk will not end in the manner I hope. If so, I can be assured that He will get me "home."

Second, the same surrendering required at the start of this walk is required on every part of this walk. It is not a one-time-and-I'm-done-thing or a-now-and-then-never-again-proposition. It is daily. The invitation from Jesus is a routine and regular submission. As strange as it sounds the upside-down nature of the Kingdom of God requires that we die daily to ourselves in order to walk daily with Him. Jesus said, "…Whoever wants to save his life will lose it, but whoever loses his life for me will find it" (Matthew 16:25). Clear? The second vital question is this. Am I learning to die daily to myself? The health of my walk depends upon it.

Third, at the very core of all that the Holy Spirit uses to change us into looking more and more like Jesus – what this study has called "various means" – how we respond to the pain, the heartaches, and tests of life can determine whether we finish the walk well or not. Failure to embrace the suffering that inevitably comes to all of us can derail and even bring our walk to a crashing halt. The grand disappointment of life is not the pain that finds us on our journey, but rather how much we miss while trying to "get away" from that pain that is tragic. So many wise spiritual directors have encouraged us to not waste our sorrows. The failure to see pain as a genuine gift from God, as difficult as that is, is a failure to believe in the goodness and grace of God at work to form us into the likeness of Jesus. All the grit and dog-eared-determination cannot get us through these seasons of pain. Only the indwelling presence of Jesus and His grace can see us to the end of our walk. Remember, He endured the cross for us, so that we would not grow weary and lose heart on the way (Hebrews 12:3). Several questions can be asked. Am I remaining teachable? Do I have a "listening spirituality?" Does my everyday theology include the cross? Do I see the grace of God at work, regardless of the circumstances, empowering me to finish well? Always be on the alert to suffering that blooms into self-pity.

Fourth, this walk requires our participation and partnership. I know for many of us that is a given, but often this long obedience in the same direction can become a sleep-walking experience. Don't overlook the power "of our cooperation." Effort, focus, resolve, and a whole host of other word pictures help to remind us of the needed involvement that is required of each of us. No exceptions. As helpful as others are to our walk with Jesus, each of us must eventually walk. Yes, there may be times when another Christian friend picks us up and carries us along the way, but the entire journey cannot be completed in that manner. We jeopardize our own vitality and that of our friend if we simply allow them to do all the cooperating. Here's the question. Have I embraced the necessary Christian disciplines that will assist me to finish well?

Fifth, humble confidence in this walk is based upon the firm promise of God to change us to look like Jesus. We are a holy work in progress (Philippians 1:6). He is "morphing" us day by day to not only look like Him, but finish like Him. Question: Do I trust that I am "being transformed into His likeness with ever-increasing glory, which comes from the Lord, who is the Spirit" (2 Corinthians 3:16)?

Sixth, no one gets very far in this walk without coming face to face with the example of Jesus in serving others (Mark 10:44-45). So much of our health and vitality in the journey depends upon our serving others in the Name of Jesus and with His grace and energy. Spiritual formation, without this central piece, is simply selfish and non-biblical. Here we discover another paradoxical truth of the Kingdom: as we give ourselves away to others we find ourselves. The question here is simple: Do I really love people in Jesus' Name? My answer to that question is central to completing the walk as a servant in the manner He intended (John 13:34-35).

Seventh and finally, the entire walk is about God. "Glory" is the word and praise of Him is the way. Our walk is to Him, for Him, with Him, through Him, in Him, beside Him, and always about Him. "To Him who sits on the throne and to the Lamb be praise and honor and glory and power, forever and ever" (Revelation 5:13)! He, for His own praise and glory, will get us home. Walk on.

J.K. Jones

Pastor of Spiritual Formation, Normal, IL